HMH

math expressions
Common Core

Dr. Karen C. Fuson

Watch the seahorse come alive in its underwater world as you discover and solve math challenges.
Download the *Math Worlds AR* app available on Android or iOS devices.

Grade **K**

Volume 1

This material is based upon work supported by the
National Science Foundation
under Grant Numbers
ESI-9816320, REC-9806020, and RED-935373.

Any opinions, findings, and conclusions, or recommendations expressed in this material
are those of the author and do not necessarily reflect the views of the National Science Foundation.

Printed in the U.S.A.

ISBN   978-0-544-91978-5

12 13 14 15 16 0607 25 24 23 22

4500851009   D E F G

BIG IDEA 3 - Show Numbers 1 Through 10

BIG IDEA 4 - Practice Numbers 1 Through 10

BIG IDEA 4 - Build Teen Numbers

Student Resources

Dear Family:

Your child is learning math in an innovative program that weaves abstract mathematical concepts with the everyday experiences of children. This helps children understand math better.

Your child will have homework. He or she needs a **Homework Helper**. The helper may be anyone—you, an older brother or sister (or other family member), a neighbor, or a friend. Make a specific time for homework and provide your child with a quiet place to work (for example, no TV). Encourage your child to talk about what is happening in math class. If your child is having problems with math, please contact me to see how you might help.

Thank you! You are vital to your child's learning.

Sincerely,
Your child's teacher

Please fill out the following information and return this form to the teacher.

My child _____ will have _____
          (child's name)   (Homework Helper's name)

as his or her Homework Helper. This person is my child's

_____.
   (relationship to child: father,
   mother, sibling, friend, etc.)

CC SS Unit 1 addresses the following standards from the Common Core State Standards for Mathematics: **K.CC.A.1, K.CC.A.3, K.CC.B.4, K.CC.B.4.a, K.CC.B.4.b, K.CC.B.5, K.CC.C.6, K.CC.C.7, K.OA.A.1, K.OA.A.2, K.MD.B.3, K.G.A.1, K.G.A.2, K.G.A.3, K.G.B.4, K.G.B.5, and all** Mathematical Practices.

Estimada familia:

Su niño está aprendiendo matemáticas con un programa innovador que relaciona conceptos matemáticos abstractos con la experiencia diaria de los niños. Esto ayuda a los niños a entender mejor las matemáticas.

Su niño tendrá tarea y necesita a una persona que lo ayude. Esa persona puede ser usted, un hermano mayor (u otro familiar), un vecino o un amigo. Establezca una hora para la tarea y ofrezca a su niño un lugar tranquilo donde trabajar (por ejemplo un lugar sin TV). Anime a su niño a comentar lo que está aprendiendo en la clase de matemáticas. Si su niño tiene problemas con las matemáticas, por favor hable con el maestro para ver cómo usted puede ayudar.

Muchas gracias. Usted es imprescindible en el aprendizaje de su niño.

Atentamente,
El maestro de su niño

Por favor complete la siguiente información y devuelva este formulario al maestro.

La persona que ayudará a mi niño _____ es
                                    (nombre del niño)

_____. Esta persona es _____
        (nombre de la persona)   (relación con el niño)

de mi niño.

© Houghton Mifflin Harcourt Publishing Company

En la Unidad 1 se aplican los siguientes estándares de los Estándares estatales comunes de matemáticas: **K.CC.A.1, K.CC.A.3, K.CC.B.4, K.CC.B.4.a, K.CC.B.4.b, K.CC.B.5, K.CC.C.6, K.CC.C.7, K.OA.A.1, K.OA.A.2, K.MD.B.3, K.G.A.1, K.G.A.2, K.G.A.3, K.G.B.4, K.G.B.5 y todos los de** Prácticas matemáticas.

above

fewer

circle

five

count

four

There are **fewer** blue tiles than red tiles.

The bird is **above** the tree.

5

4

greater

in front of

group

larger

how many

left

The girl is **in front of** the fence.

3   5

↑

greater

↑

larger

This **group** has 3 circles.

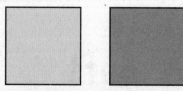

The yellow square is on the **left**.

Examples:

How many fingers? 5 fingers

less	order
more	rectangle
one	right

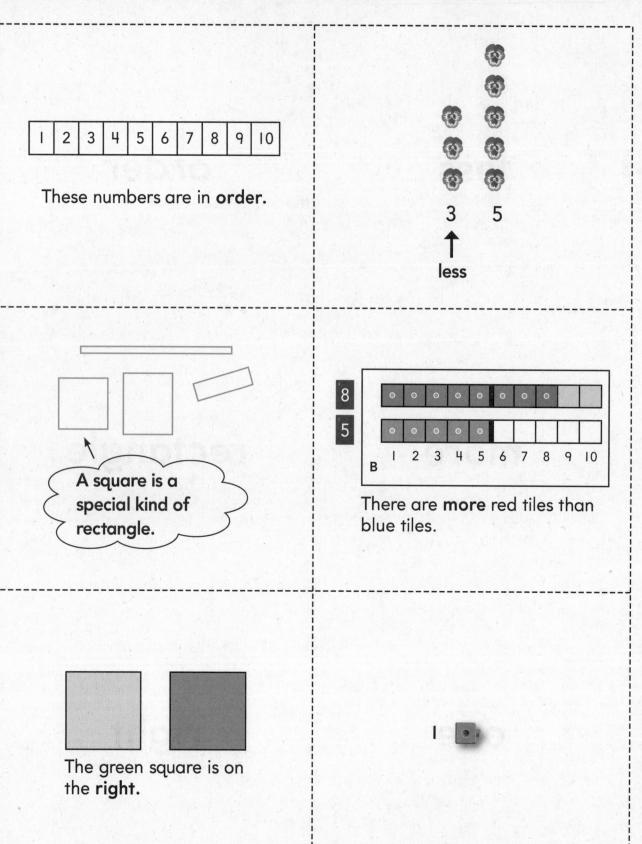

| 1 | 2 | 3 | 4 | 5 | 6 | 7 | 8 | 9 | 10 |

These numbers are in **order**.

3   5

↑
less

A square is a special kind of rectangle.

8

5

1 2 3 4 5 6 7 8 9 10

B

There are **more** red tiles than blue tiles.

The green square is on the **right**.

1

side

three

smaller

two

square

zero

3 ◼◼◼

◀ side

2 ◼◼

smaller

0

There are **zero** apples on the plate.

© Houghton Mifflin Harcourt Publishing Company

Draw a ring around 1 barn.

Draw a ring around 2 chickens.

Draw a ring around 3 cows.

Draw a ring around 2 slides.

Draw a ring around 4 swings.

Draw a ring around 5 children.

✔ Check Understanding

TEACHER: Count the number of birds and tell how many.

Introduce Number and Counting Routines

1	2	3	4	5	6
1	2	3	4	5	6

7	8	9	10
7	8	9	10

Number Tiles and Square-Inch Tiles **5**

Number Tiles and Square-Inch Tiles

Name _____

Draw a line. Match the Number Tile to the same number of squares.

1

2

3

4

5

Ring the **groups** of tiles that match the Number Tile.

4

4

✔ **Check Understanding**

TEACHER: Draw books to show each number.

3

5

Relate Objects and Numbers Through 5

Dear Family:

Your child has just read and discussed *Anno's Counting Book*. This book is an introduction to beginning numbers. It is filled with charming scenes that show many things all of the same number (for example, a scene showing many different groups of 3 things). Each page shows a month of the year.

We have discussed what a scene is in class. *A scene is a place where some action or event occurs, a picture*. The children will be making their own scenes or pictures. Sometimes this will be started in class and completed for homework. You can help by talking with your child about what he or she might draw, for example, your child might draw 2 of something, such as things found in a kitchen—2 plates, 2 bowls, 2 spoons.

Help your child practice counting things in daily life. Children might count how many stairs there are in your home, how many plates you need to set the table, or how many people are in the family.

Thank you for helping your child learn more about numbers and counting!

Sincerely,
Your child's teacher

CC SS Unit 1 addresses the following standards from the Common Core State Standards for Mathematics: **K.CC.A.1, K.CC.A.3, K.CC.B.4, K.CC.B.4.a, K.CC.B.4.b, K.CC.B.5, K.CC.C.6, K.CC.C.7, K.OA.A.1, K.OA.A.2, K.MD.B.3, K.G.A.1, K.G.A.2, K.G.A.3, K.G.B.4, K.G.B.5,** and all Mathematical Practices.

Estimada familia:

Su niño acaba de leer y comentar un libro para contar. Este libro es una introducción a los primeros números. Está lleno de escenas fascinantes que muestran muchas cosas, todas acerca de los mismos números (por ejemplo, una escena muestra varios grupos diferentes de 3 cosas). Cada página indica un mes del año.

Hemos comentado en clase lo que es una escena. *Una escena es un lugar donde ocurre una acción o un suceso, un dibujo.* Los niños van a hacer sus propias escenas o dibujos. A veces los empezarán en clase y los terminarán de tarea. Usted puede ayudar hablando con su niño sobre lo que puede dibujar. Por ejemplo: si va a dibujar 2 de algo, podría dibujar cosas que están en la cocina, 2 platos, 2 tazones, 2 cucharas.

Ayude a su niño a practicar contando cosas que usen a diario. Los niños pueden contar cuántas escaleras hay en su casa, cuántos platos se necesitan para poner la mesa o cuántas personas hay en la familia.

¡Gracias por ayudar a su niño a aprender más sobre los números y a contar!

Atentamente,
El maestro de su niño

En la Unidad 1 se aplican los siguientes estándares de los Estándares estatales comunes de matemáticas: **K.CC.A.1, K.CC.A.3, K.CC.B.4, K.CC.B.4.a, K.CC.B.4.b, K.CC.B.5, K.CC.C.6, K.CC.C.7, K.OA.A.1, K.OA.A.2, K.MD.B.3, K.G.A.1, K.G.A.2, K.G.A.3, K.G.B.4, K.G.B.5 y todos los de** Prácticas matemáticas.

Name _____

Draw a scene with groups of 2.

Draw a scene with groups of 3.

 Check Understanding

TEACHER: Ring the number to show how many are in each group.

1   2   3   1   2   3

Draw Scenes of 2 and 3

Find groups of 3.

Color the objects that are in groups of 3.

Find groups of 2.

Color the objects that are in groups of 2.

✔ **Check Understanding**

TEACHER: Place 3 Square-Inch tiles in a row as shown. Now move the tiles so the group looks different. Draw to show what the new group looks like.

Counting and Cardinality 1–5

Name _____

Draw a scene with groups of 4.

Draw a scene with groups of 5.

✔ Check Understanding

TEACHER: Draw 4 apples. Draw 4 oranges. Count the apples. Tell how many.
Count the oranges. Tell how many.

4 apples	4 oranges

Counting and Cardinality Through 5

Name _____

Look at the picture.
How many cats are there?

Look at what Puzzled Penguin wrote.

Help Puzzled Penguin.

I cat

Am I correct?

Count the cats.
Ring the number of cats.

0   2

Count the dogs.
Ring the number of dogs.

3   5

© Houghton Mifflin Harcourt Publishing Company

Draw 5 hats.

Draw 3 cats.

Draw 4 stars.

Draw 2 cars.

✔ Check Understanding

TEACHER: Count the balls. Ring the number.

3   4   5

Name _____

VOCABULARY
how many

Put out 1 red square.

Put out 2 blue squares.

Draw to show **how many** squares in all.

Put out 2 red squares.

Put out 2 blue squares.

Draw to show how many squares in all.

Content Standards K.CC.B.4, K.CC.B.4.a, K.CC.B.4.b, K.CC.B.5, K.OA.A.1, K.OA.A.2
Mathematical Practices MP4

Put out 5 red squares.

Take away 2 squares.

Draw to show how many squares are left.

Put out 4 red squares.

Take away 3 squares.

Draw to show how many squares are left.

✔ Check Understanding

TEACHER: Clap to show how many red squares. Clap to show how many blue squares. How many squares are there in all?

　　　　　　　　　　　　Introduce Adding and Subtracting

Circles

Circles

VOCABULARY
circle

Trace each **circle**.
Color the circles.

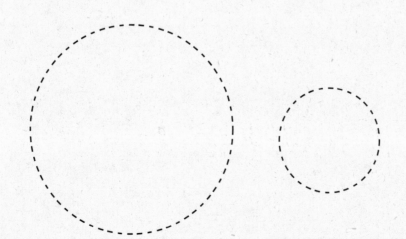

Look at the red circle.

Draw two circles that are **larger**.

Draw two circles that are **smaller**.

Color the circles different colors.

VOCABULARY
larger
smaller

✓ **Check Understanding**

TEACHER: Choose 2 of the circles you drew above. How are they alike? How are they different?

　　　　　　　　　　　　　　　　　　　　Identify Circles

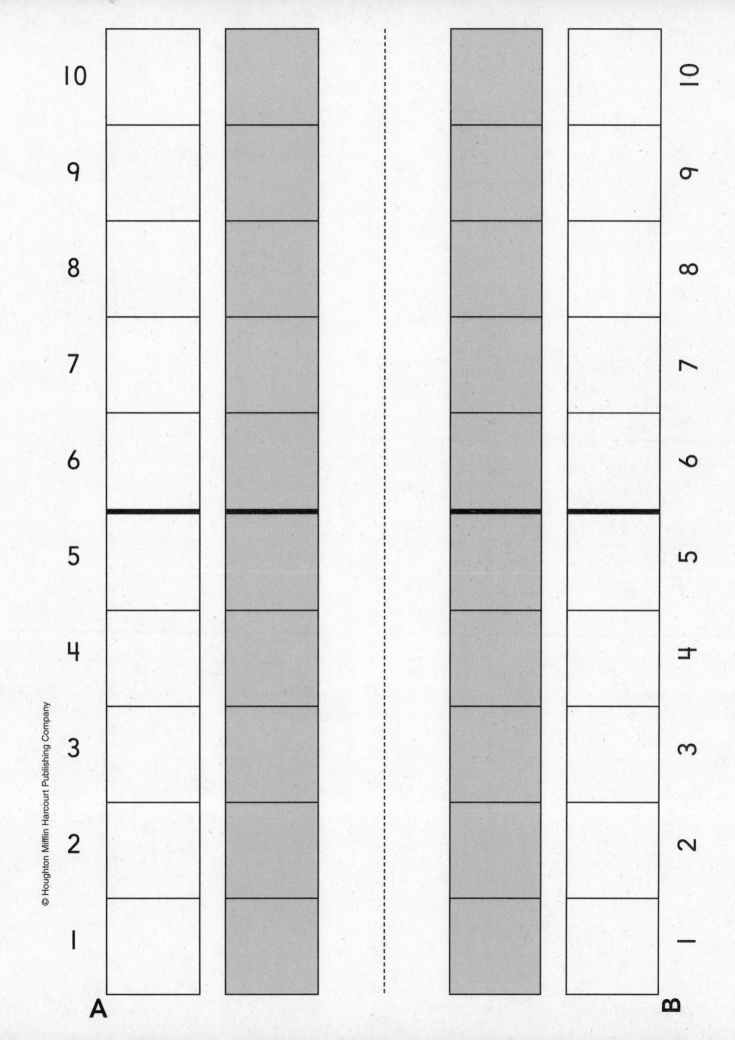

A

10
9
8
7
6
5
4
3
2
1

B

10
9
8
7
6
5
4
3
2
1

Comparing Mat

Name _____

VOCABULARY
less
greater

Look at the comparing mat.

Ring the number that is **less**.

3   5

Ring the number that is **greater**.

4   2

Color to show each number.

Ring the number that is greater.

1   4

Ring the number that is less.

5   2

✔ Check Understanding

TEACHER: Use Comparing Mat B. Put 3 tiles on the top row and 1 in the bottom row. Explain what it shows.

Introduce Comparing

Squares and Rectangles

Squares and Rectangles

VOCABULARY
square

Color each circle yellow. Color each **square** blue.
Draw a face under your favorite hat.

Color each kind of shape as shown.

VOCABULARY
rectangle

circle   square   **rectangle**

✔ Check Understanding

TEACHER: Look at the green shape. Ring the name of the shape.

circle

square

rectangle

Identify Squares and Rectangles

Name _____

Color to show each number.
Ring the tower with **fewer**.

Color to show each number.
Ring the tower with **more**.

6   7

10
9
8
7
6
5
4
3
2
1
A

9   5

10
9
8
7
6
5
4
3
2
1
A

Content Standards K.CC.B.4, K.CC.B.4.a, K.CC.B.4.b, K.CC.B.5, K.CC.C.6
Mathematical Practices MP4, MP6

Sal says the row with 9 has more.

Jenna says the row with 8 has more.

Who is correct? Ring your answer.   Sal   Jenna

Ava says the row with 7 has fewer.

Jin says the row with 5 has fewer.

Who is correct? Ring your answer.   Ava   Jin

✓ Check Understanding

TEACHER: What does this picture show?

Count from 1 to 10

Dear Family:

Your child is learning to write numbers. You might notice that sometimes your child might write numbers backwards or reverse them. This is very common in early number writing. You can ask your child, "Does this number look OK?" Then point out that it is written backwards. Eventually our goal is that children may identify their own reversals, write correct numbers, and write faster in preparation for first grade.

Thank you!

Sincerely,
Your child's teacher

Unit 1 addresses the following standards from the Common Core State Standards for Mathematics: **K.CC.A.1, K.CC.A.3, K.CC.B.4, K.CC.B.4.a, K.CC.B.4.b, K.CC.B.5, K.CC.C.6, K.CC.C.7, K.OA.A.1, K.OA.A.2, K.MD.B.3, K.G.A.1, K.G.A.2, K.G.A.3, K.G.B.4, K.G.B.5,** and all Mathematical Practices.

Estimada familia:

Su niño está aprendiendo a escribir los números. Usted observará que a veces su niño escribe los números al revés o que los invierte. Esto es normal al empezar a escribir los números. Puede preguntarle, "¿Está bien escrito este número?" Luego indíquele que está escrito al revés. Nuestro objetivo es que, más adelante, los niños se den cuenta de que han invertido los números, que los escriban correctamente y que escriban más rápido para prepararse para el primer grado.

¡Gracias!

Atentamente,
El maestro de su niño

CC SS **En la Unidad 1 se aplican los siguientes estándares de los** Estándares estatales comunes de matemáticas: **K.CC.A.1, K.CC.A.3, K.CC.B.4, K.CC.B.4.a, K.CC.B.4.b, K.CC.B.5, K.CC.C.6, K.CC.C.7, K.OA.A.1, K.OA.A.2, K.MD.B.3, K.G.A.1, K.G.A.2, K.G.A.3, K.G.B.4, K.G.B.5 y todos los de** Prácticas matemáticas.

Name _____

Write the numbers.

1

1

1

1

1

2 2 2 2 2 2 2 2

2

2

2

Write the number 3.

3 3 3 3 3 3 3 3

3

3 3 3

3

Draw 3 objects.	Draw 3 circles.

✔ Check Understanding

TEACHER: Without counting the tiles, how does the Comparing Mat help you know which group has more tiles than the other?

Objects and Numbers Through 10

Go left to right.

Ring groups of the number.

Mark an X on the groups that are not the number.

3　　　　

4　　　　

5　　　　

2　　　　

Content Standards **K.CC.A.3, K.CC.B.4, K.CC.B.4.a, K.CC.B.4.b**
Mathematical Practices **MP6**

Draw 3 rectangles.

Write the number 3.

3 3 3 3 3 3 3 3

3

3   3   3

✔ **Check Understanding**

© Houghton Mifflin Harcourt Publishing Company

TEACHER: Draw 3 apples. Then draw 3 apples another way.

Practice Numbers 1–10

Name _____

Write the number 4.

Draw 4 objects.	Draw 4 rectangles.

Content Standards K.CC.A.3, K.CC.B.4, K.CC.B.4.a, K.CC.B.4.b, K.CC.B.5, K.OA.A.1, K.OA.A.2 **Mathematical Practices** MP2, MP4, MP8

Numbers of Objects in a Group **41**

Trace the number 4. Color each group of 4 a different color.
Mark an X on the objects that are not in a group of 4.

Numbers of Objects in a Group

Name _____

Tell an adding story.

First   Then   At the end

1

2

Tell a subtracting story.

First   Then   At the end

3

4

Numbers of Objects in a Group **43**

Tell math stories about the pictures.

 Check Understanding

TEACHER: Draw a picture of 3 red balls and 1 green ball. Tell a story.

Numbers of Objects in a Group

Name _____

Puzzled Penguin compared numbers.

Puzzled Penguin showed the numbers.

Then Puzzled Penguin drew a ring around
the number that is greater. Help Puzzled Penguin.

Am I correct?

A ⑥   8

⑨   7 B

Go left to right. Ring groups of the number. Mark an X on the groups that are not the number.

3

4

5

2

✔ **Check Understanding**

TEACHER: Without counting each dot, how many dots do you see? How do you know?

Objects and Numbers Through 10

Name _____

Write the number 5.

5　5　5　5　5　5　5　5

5

5　　　5　　　5

5

5

Draw 5 objects.	Draw 5 squares.

Count the animals. Ring the number. Then color each group a different color.

2   3   4   5

2   3   4   5

2   3   4   5

2   3   4   5

Write the number 0.

✓ Check Understanding

TEACHER: Draw a group of 4 dots. Draw another group with fewer dots.

© Houghton Mifflin Harcourt Publishing Company

Practice: Number of Objects in a Group

Connect the dots in **order**.

Write the numbers.

1 1 1 1 1 1 1 1

2 2 2 2 2 2 2 2

2 ʔ ʔ ʔ ʔ ʔ ʔ ʔ

3 3 3 3 3 3 3 3

3 ʔ ʔ ʔ ʔ ʔ ʔ ʔ

4 4 4 4 4 4 4 4

4 4 4 4 4 4 4 4

5 5 5 5 5 5 5 5

5 5 5 5 5 5 5 5

✓ Check Understanding

TEACHER: What number comes next? Write the number in the box.

1, 2, 3, ☐

More Objects and Numbers Through 10

Color shapes with 0 straight **sides** blue.
Color shapes with 4 sides red.

VOCABULARY
sides

Draw some more shapes with 0 straight sides.
Draw some more shapes with 4 sides.

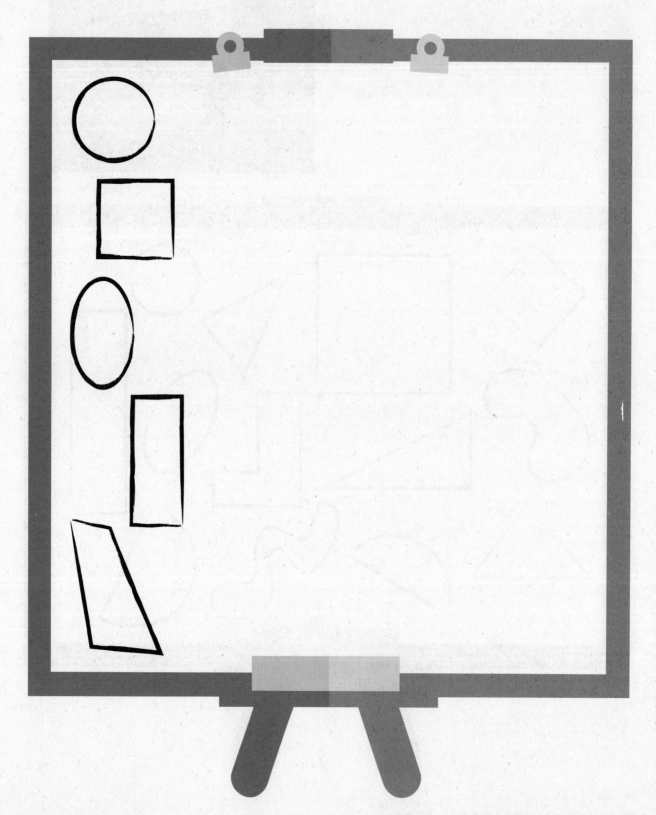

Focus on Mathematical Practices

Ring groups of the number. Mark an X on the groups that are not the number.

1

4

2

2

3 Draw 3 trees.

4 Draw 5 flowers.

5 Draw a line under each circle.

6 Draw a line under each rectangle.

7 Connect the dots in order.

8

9 Write the numbers.

10 Does the picture match the number? Choose Yes or No.

○ Yes   ○ No

11 Make a drawing. Use 1 square, 3 circles, and 4 rectangles. Did you draw fewer squares or circles? Mark an X on the shape that has fewer.

Number Train

Part A

Name

Part B

Dear Family:

Children are learning to see numbers 6, 7, 8, 9, and 10 as having a 5 and some more. This is called using a 5-group. This visual pattern will help children add, subtract, and understand numbers. It will also help later in multidigit calculation.

Count things at home in 5-groups to help your child see the 5 in 6, 7, 8, 9, and 10. For example, 7 buttons can be counted using 5-groups: "5 and 2 make 7."

Children will see 5-groups in materials they are using in school:

Number Parade

Square-Inch Tiles

Counters and 5-Counter Strips

Thank you!

Sincerely,
Your child's teacher

CC SS Unit 2 addresses the following standards from the Common Core State Standards for Mathematics: **K.CC.A.1, K.CC.A.2, K.CC.A.3, K.CC.B.4, K.CC.B.4.a, K.CC.B.4.b, K.CC.B.4.c, K.CC.B.5, K.CC.C.6, K.CC.C.7, K.OA.A.1, K.OA.A.2, K.OA.A.3, K.NBT.A.1, K.MD.B.3, K.G.A.1, K.G.A.2, K.G.A.3, K.G.B.4,** and all Mathematical Practices.

Estimada familia:

Los niños están aprendiendo a ver que los números 6, 7, 8, 9 y 10 contienen el 5 y algo más. Esto se llama usar un grupo de 5. Este patrón visual los ayudará a sumar, a restar y a entender los números. Más adelante también les servirá para los cálculos con números de más de un dígito.

Cuenten cosas en casa haciendo grupos de 5 para que el niño identifique el 5 en el 6, 7, 8 , 9 y 10. Por ejemplo, pueden contar 7 botones haciendo un grupo de 5: "5 más 2 son 7".

Los niños identificarán grupos de 5 en los materiales que usan en la escuela:

Desfile de números

| **6** | **7** | **8** | **9** | **10** |

Azulejos de una pulgada cuadrada

| 6 | 7 | 8 | 9 | 10 |

Fichas y tiras de 5 fichas

| 6 | 7 | 8 | 9 | 10 |

¡Muchas gracias!

Atentamente,
El maestro de su niño

En la Unidad 2 se aplican los siguientes estándares de los Estándares estatales comunes de matemáticas: **K.CC.A.1, K.CC.A.2, K.CC.A.3, K.CC.B.4.a, K.CC.B.4.b, K.CC.B.4.c, K.CC.B.5, K.CC.C.6, K.CC.C.7, K.OA.A.1, K.OA.A.2, K.OA.A.3, K.NBT.A.1, K.MD.B.3, K.G.A.1, K.G.A.2, K.G.A.3, K.G.B.4** y todos los de Prácticas matemáticas.

eight

nine

hexagon

plus (+)

minus (–)

seven

9

8

$3 + 2 = 5$
3 **plus** 2 equals 5.

7

$8 - 3 = 5$
8 **minus** 3 equals 5.

six

triangle

straight lines

ten

© Houghton Mifflin Harcourt Publishing Company

UNIT 2 Vocabulary Cards

60C

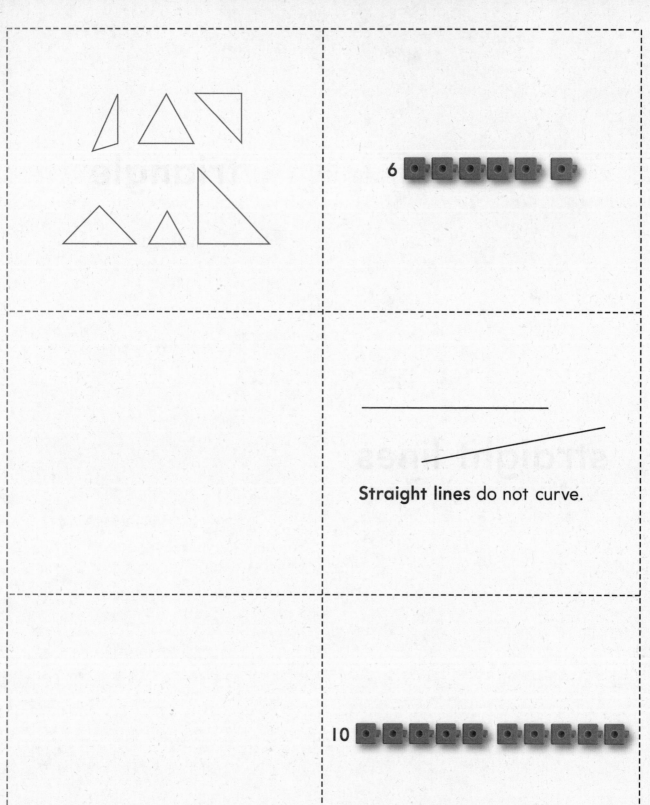

Straight lines do not curve.

Name _____

Find and color groups of 1 through 10.

CC SS Content Standards K.CC.A.3, K.CC.B.4, K.CC.B.4.a, K.CC.B.4.b, K.CC.B.5 Mathematical Practices MP3, MP6

Find Numbers 1–10: Neighborhood Scene **61**

Help Puzzled Penguin.

Did Puzzled Penguin write the numbers

I through 5 in order correctly?

Did I make a mistake?

| 1 | 2 | 4 | 3 | 5 |

Write the numbers I through 5 in order.

Write the numbers 0 through 5 in order.

✓ **Check Understanding**

TEACHER: Tell how you can find the number of butterflies. Then tell how many.

Find Numbers 1–10: Neighborhood Scene

© Houghton Mifflin Harcourt Publishing Company

Cut on dashed lines.
Do not cut on solid lines.

5-Square Tiles **63**

5-Square Tiles

Name _____

Use a 5-group. Write the number.

1

5   +   ☐

2

5   +   ☐

3

5   +   ☐

Content Standards K.CC.A.2, K.OA.A.1, K.OA.A.2
Mathematical Practices MP7

Use a 5-group. Write the number.

4

5 + ☐

5

5 + ☐

6

5 + ☐

✓ **Check Understanding**

TEACHER: What number do you need to add to a 5-group to get 8?

Relate Objects and Numbers 6–10

Name _____

Ring groups of the number. Mark an X on groups that are not the number.

6

7

8

9

10

© Houghton Mifflin Harcourt Publishing Company

CC SS Content Standards **K.CC.B.4, K.CC.B.4.a, K.CC.B.4.b, K.CC.B.5**
Mathematical Practices **MP6, MP7**

Draw dots to show the number.

6

_____

7

_____

8

_____

9

_____

10

 Check Understanding

TEACHER: Without counting, tell how many dots are in each group.
Now count aloud to check your answers.

Family Math Stories

Cut on dashed lines. Fold on solid lines and tape at top and bottom.

5

5

5

5

5

5

5-Counter Strips **69**

5-Counter Strips

Name _____

Use 5-groups.

Write the number of extra counters.

1

2

3

4

CC SS **Content Standards** K.CC.B.4, K.CC.B.4.a, K.CC.B.4.b, K.CC.B.5, K.OA.A.1
Mathematical Practices MP3, MP6

Puzzled Penguin used a 5-Counter Strip and some extra counters to show 7.

Did Puzzled Penguin make a mistake?

Help Puzzled Penguin.

Am I correct?

Draw a 5-Counter Strip and some extra counters to show 9.

✓ **Check Understanding**

TEACHER: Look at the grouping for the number 7. Why does showing a 5-group make it easier to see the number?

5-Groups in Numbers 6–10

Name _____

Write the number 6.

6   6   6   6   6   6   6   6

6

6   6   6

6

Draw 6 objects.	Draw 6 balls.

Ring 6 hats.

Write the number 6.

6   6   6   6   6   6   6   6

6

✔ Check Understanding

TEACHER: Ring the number of marbles.

6

7

8

Add and Subtract with Family Math Stories

Name _____

Tell an addition or subtraction story.

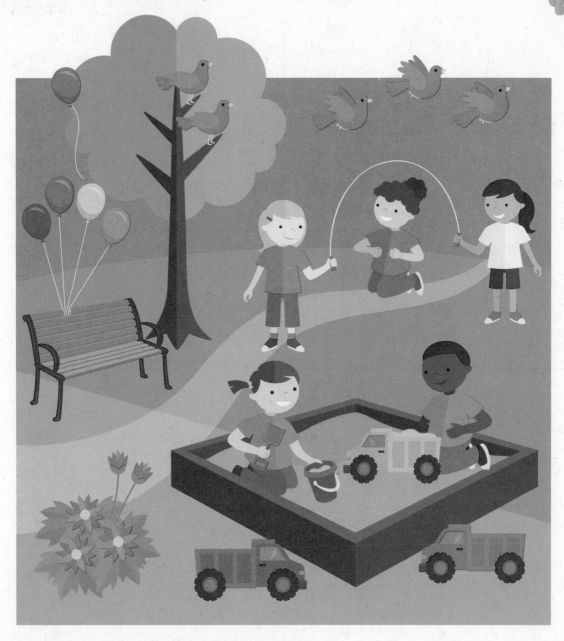

Make a drawing to show how many balloons in all.

Connect the dots in order. Use straight lines.

10   1   2   3   9   8   4   7   5   6

9   10   1   2   8   7   4   5   3   6

1   10   2   3   9   4   8   6   7   5

7   6   8   5   4   9   3   2   10   1

✓ Check Understanding

TEACHER: Draw a picture to show $1 + 3 = 4$.

Addition and Subtraction Stories: Playground Scenario

1	2	3	4	5	6
1	2	3	4	5	6

7	8	9	10
7	8	9	10

+ + + − − −

= = = ≠ ≠ ≠

© Houghton Mifflin Harcourt Publishing Company

+/− Tiles, =/≠ Tiles **77**

+/− Tiles, =/≠ Tiles

Name _____

Write the numbers 2 and 5.

2 2 2 2 2 2 2 2

2 ' ' ' ' ' ' '

2 ' ' 2 ' ' 2 '

Draw 2 objects.	Draw 2 circles.

Draw 5 objects.	Draw 5 squares.

Content Standards K.CC.A.3, K.CC.B.4
Mathematical Practices MP3, MP6

Write numbers 0 through 5 in order. Use the Number Parade to help.

0 0 0 0

1 1 1 1

2 2 2 2 2 2 2 2
2

3 3 3 3 3 3 3 3
3

4 4 4 4 4 4 4 4
4

5 5 5 5 5 5 5 5
5

 ## Check Understanding

TEACHER: Draw a set of objects to show the number 5.

Name _____

Write the number 7.

Draw 7 objects.	Draw 7 squares.

Write the numbers 0 through 7 in order.

Connect the dots in order.

✔ Check Understanding

TEACHER: Explain how you know which number to go to next for the dot-to-dot drawings.

Numbers 1–10

Name _____

Use a pencil or marker and trace each number 2 times. Use the color blue to trace the 6s and the color red to trace the 7s.

Write the numbers 1 through 7 in order.

Content Standards **K.CC.A.2, K.CC.A.3**
Mathematical Practices **MP2**

Help Puzzled Penguin.

Did Puzzled Penguin make a mistake?

Look at the numbers below.

Did I make a mistake?

4	3	6	7	5

Write the numbers 3 through 7 in order.

Write the numbers 0 through 7 in order.

 Check Understanding

TEACHER: Draw a set of 7 objects.

Practice with 5-Groups

Name _____

Write the number 8.

Draw 8 objects.

Draw 8 rectangles.

Ring 8 objects.

Write the number 8.

✔ Check Understanding

TEACHER: Four squirrels are in a tree. Two squirrels are on the ground.
Ring to show how many squirrels there are in all.

4   6   8

Numbers 6, 7, and 8

Name _____

Tell a math story.

The Neighborhood
GARDEN

Write the number 9.

Draw 9 objects.	Draw 9 circles.

✓ **Check Understanding**

TEACHER: Draw to show how many in all.

5 + 2

Addition and Subtraction Stories: Garden Scenario

Look at the counters.
Write the missing numbers.

1

☐ + 1 = ☐

2

☐ + 1 = ☐

3

☐ + 1 = ☐

Content Standards **K.CC.B.5, K.OA.A.1, K.OA.A.2**
Mathematical Practices **MP6**

Draw circles to show the numbers.

How many in all?

Write the number.

$$4 \quad + \quad 1 \quad = \quad \boxed{}$$

5

$$5 \quad + \quad 1 \quad = \quad \boxed{}$$

 Check Understanding

TEACHER: Explain how you can use counters to show 7 + 1. Then solve.

Numbers 1 Through 10: The +1 Pattern

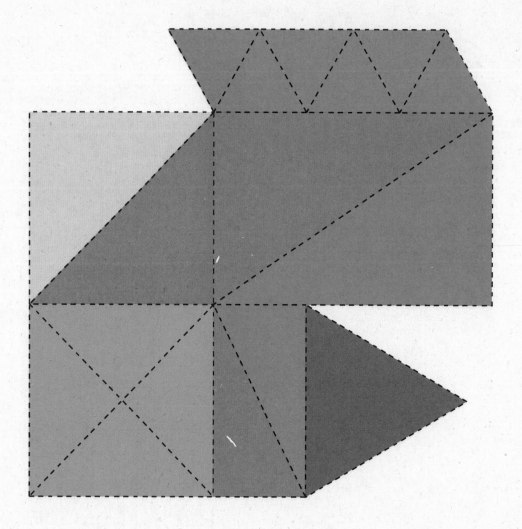

Triangles

Name _____

VOCABULARY
triangle

Discuss shapes you see.

Trace the shapes.

Draw the same shapes below the pictures.

Color the **triangles** you draw.

Name shapes you see.

Count the sides of each shape.

Color each shape needed to build the doghouse above.

✔ Check Understanding

TEACHER: Tell how many sides a triangle has.
Tell how many corners a triangle has.

Identify Triangles

Name _____

Look at the counters.

Write the missing numbers.

 1

◻ + 1 = ◻

2

◻ + 1 = ◻

Look at the counters.

Write the missing numbers.

 3

☐ + 1 = ☐

 4

☐ + 1 = ☐

 ✔ **Check Understanding**

TEACHER: Draw counters to show a +1 equation, and use Number Tiles to show the equation .

More Numbers 1 Through 10: The +1 Pattern

Name _____

Write the number 10.

Draw 10 triangles.	Draw 10 circles.

Ring 10 fish.

Practice writing the number 10.

✓ **Check Understanding**

TEACHER: How many shovels are there? Write the number.

Addition and Subtraction Stories: Family Experiences

Name _____

Use counters. Take away 1.

Write the number.

---

1 $10 - 1 = \boxed{}$ **2** $9 - 1 = \boxed{}$

3 $8 - 1 = \boxed{}$ **4** $7 - 1 = \boxed{}$

5 $6 - 1 = \boxed{}$ **6** $5 - 1 = \boxed{}$

Use counters. Take away 1.

Write the number.

7 4 − 1 = ☐

8 3 − 1 = ☐

9 2 − 1 = ☐

10 1 − 1 = ☐

✔ **Check Understanding**

TEACHER: Explain how to solve a −1 equation.

8 − 1 = 7

Numbers 1 Through 10: The −1 Pattern

Hexagons

Identify Hexagons **103**

Identify Hexagons

Name _____

VOCABULARY
hexagon

Color the shapes of one kind the same color as shown below.

circle   triangle   square   **hexagon**   rectangle

Tell which shapes can have more than one color? Why?

Check Understanding

TEACHER: What are some different words we can use to describe the position of shapes?

Identify Hexagons

Name _____

Use a pencil or marker.
Trace each number two times.
Use the color red to trace the 8s.
Use the color blue to trace the 9s.

Write the numbers 1 through 10 in order.

CC SS Content Standards **K.CC.A.1, K.CC.A.2, K.CC.A.3** Mathematical Practices **MP3, MP6**

Help Puzzled Penguin.

Puzzled Penguin was asked to write the number 6.

Did Puzzled Penguin write the number correctly?

Am I correct?

What number did Puzzled Penguin write?

How can we help Puzzled Penguin write the correct number?

Write the number for Puzzled Penguin.

Practice writing the number 6.

Practice writing the number 9.

Write the numbers 6 through 10 in order.

 Check Understanding

TEACHER: Write the number 6. Draw a group of objects to show the number.

Number Writing Practice

Name _____

Help Puzzled Penguin.

Did Puzzled Penguin make a mistake?

Look at the numbers below.

Did I make a mistake?

Cross out any numbers that are not in the correct order.

1	2	3	4	5	7	6	8	9	10

Help Puzzled Penguin write the numbers in the correct order.

Cross out any numbers that are not in the correct order.

0	1	2	3	4	5	6	7	9	8

Help Puzzled Penguin write the numbers in the correct order.

Write the numbers 1 through 10 in order.

| 1 | 2 | | 4 | | | 7 | | | 10 |

| | 2 | 3 | | 5 | 6 | | 8 | 9 | |

| | | | | | | | | | |

Write the numbers 0 through 9 in order.

| 0 | 1 | | 3 | 4 | | | 7 | | 9 |

| 0 | | 2 | | | 5 | 6 | | 8 | |

| | | | | | | | | | |

 ## Check Understanding

TEACHER: Tell which number comes before 6.

Tell which number comes after 7.

More Numbers 1 Through 10: The –1 Pattern

Name _____

Color the shapes of one kind the same color.
Count the number of each shape.
Write the number.

Draw a line to match each shape below to a shape in the picture.

circle   rectangle   triangle   square

Focus on Mathematical Practices

1 Choose all the groups of the number.

○   ○   ○

---

2 Does the set show 7? Choose Yes or No.

○ Yes   ○ No

○ Yes   ○ No

○ Yes   ○ No

Connect the dots in order.

3

4

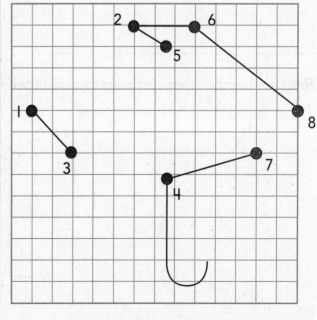

5 Ring the 5-group. Count the total. Write the number.

$$5 + 1 = \boxed{}$$

---

6 Draw a line through one circle to show 9 take away 1. Write the answer.

Ring the number that completes the number sentence.

$$9 - 1 = \begin{array}{|c|} \hline 7 \\ 8 \\ 9 \\ \hline \end{array}$$

7 Draw 4 triangles in the box. Write how many sides a triangle has.

A triangle has ⬚ sides.

---

8 Draw a line under each hexagon.

Name _____ Date _____

9 Look at the number tiles. Write the numbers 6 through 10 in order.

---

10 Draw a picture that shows 6 + 1 triangles.
Write how many triangles.

Name _____

Train Stories

Part A

[ ]

[ ]

Part B

5 = ☐ + ☐

5 − ☐ = ☐

Dear Family:

Your child is starting a new unit on grouping concepts. These concepts provide a foundation for understanding basic math equations. In class, children will learn to find the ten in teen numbers ($17 = 10 + 7$), break apart numbers to find "partners" ($6 = 4 + 2$), recognize when numbers are equal or not equal, apply the concepts of *more* and *fewer*, and observe different attributes of shapes.

Being able to group numbers and shapes makes them easier to understand. You can help your child by practicing grouping concepts at home. Here is an example of an activity you can do with your child:

When cleaning up from play, have your child sort the objects before putting them away. Talk about the differences in size, shape, and color, and help your child place the items in groups based on these attributes. For example, the blocks below are sorted by size. They could also be sorted by color.

Thank you for your continued support.

Sincerely,
Your child's teacher

CC SS Unit 3 addresses the following standards from the Common Core State Standards for Mathematics: **K.CC.A.1, K.CC.A.2, K.CC.A.3, K.CC.B.4, K.CC.B.4.a, K.CC.B.4.b, K.CC.B.4.c, K.CC.B.5, K.CC.C.6, K.CC.C.7, K.OA.A.1, K.OA.A.2, K.OA.A.3, K.OA.A.5, K.NBT.A.1, K.MD.B.3, K.G.A.1, K.G.A.2, K.G.B.4, K.G.B.5, K.G.B.6, and all** Mathematical Practices.

Estimada familia:

Su niño está empezando una nueva unidad que trata sobre los conceptos de agrupar. Estos conceptos son muy importantes para comprender las ecuaciones matemáticas básicas. Los niños aprenderán a hallar la decena en los números de 11 a 19 (17 = 10 + 7), a separar números para hallar "partes" (6 = 4 + 2), a reconocer si los números son iguales o no, a aplicar los conceptos de *más* y *menos* y a observar las características de las figuras.

Agrupar números y figuras facilita su comprensión. Usted puede ayudar a su niño practicando en casa los conceptos de agrupar. Aquí tiene un ejemplo de una actividad que pueden hacer:

Cuando estén guardando las cosas después de jugar, pida a su niño que separe los objetos en categorías. Háblele de las diferencias de tamaño, forma y color, y ayúdelo a colocar los objetos en grupos según estas características. Por ejemplo, los bloques que aparecen a continuación están agrupados según su tamaño. También se pueden agrupar según su color.

Gracias por su apoyo.

Atentamente,
El maestro de su niño

CC SS **En la Unidad 3 se aplican los siguientes estándares de los** Estándares estatales comunes de matemáticas: **K.CC.A.1, K.CC.A.2, K.CC.A.3, K.CC.B.4, K.CC.B.4.a, K.CC.B.4.b, K.CC.B.4.c, K.CC.B.5, K.CC.C.6, K.CC.C.7, K.OA.A.1, K.OA.A.2, K.OA.A.3, K.OA.A.5, K.NBT.A.1, K.MD.B.3, K.G.A.1, K.G.A.2, K.G.B.4, K.G.B.5, K.G.B.6 y todos los de** Prácticas matemáticas.

add

beside

behind

classify

below

equal to sign
(=)

The slide is **beside** the tree.

$$3 + 2 = 5$$

apples

not apples

The boy is **behind** the fence.

$$4 + 4 = 8$$
4 plus 4 **is equal to** 8.

The tree is **below** the bird.

next to	subtract
not equal to sign (≠)	teen numbers
sort	total

$8 - 3 = 5$

◯◯◯◯◯ ◯◯◯

The tree is **next to** the slide.

11 12 13 14 15 16 17 18 19

$6 \neq 8$

6 is **not equal to** 8.

$4 + 3 = 7$

↑

total

You can **sort** animals into groups.

unknown

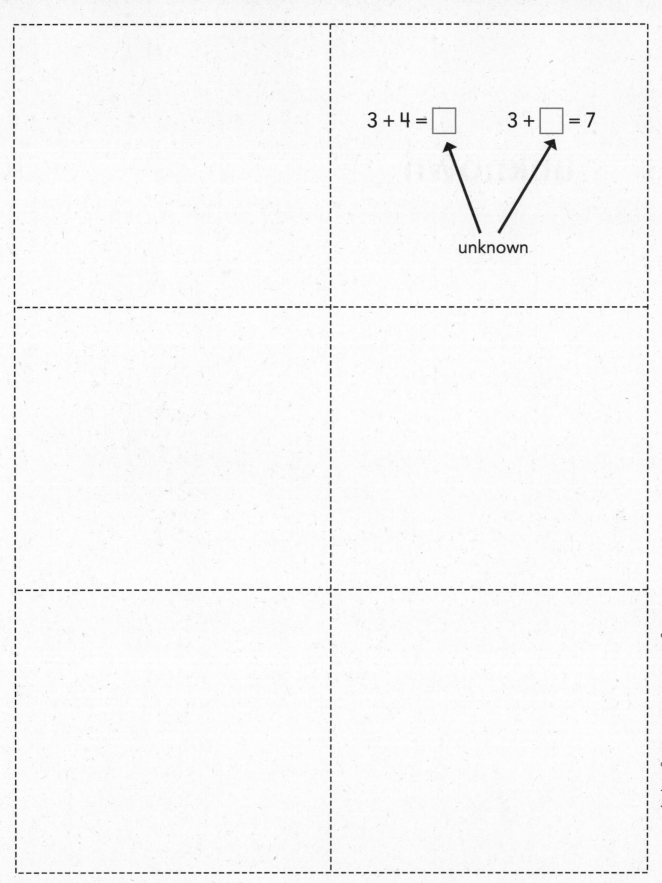

$$3 + 4 = \boxed{} \qquad 3 + \boxed{} = 7$$

unknown

Name _____

Color each group of 1 through 10 a different color.

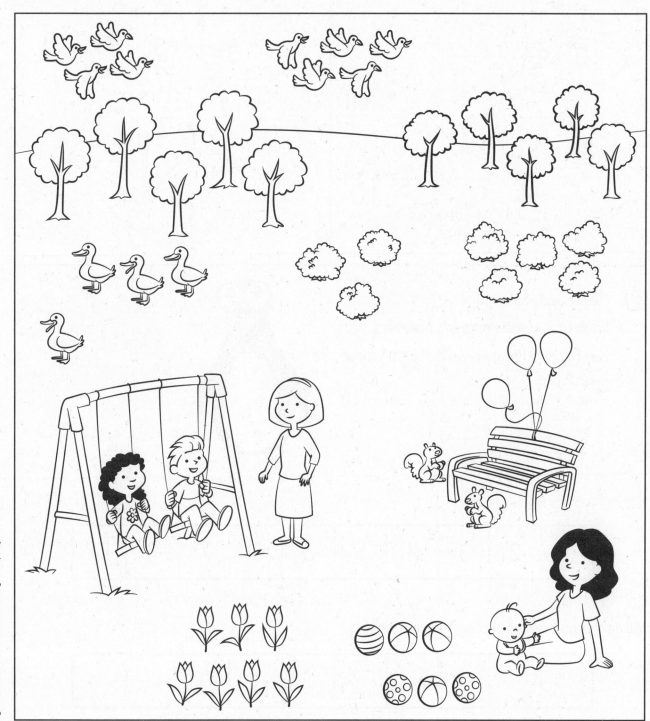

1 Connect the dots in order.

2 Help Puzzled Penguin.

Look at Puzzled Penguin's numbers.
Did Puzzled Penguin write the numbers
in order?

Am I correct?

1	2	3	4	5	6	8	7	9	10

Write the numbers 1 through 10 in order.

 Check Understanding

TEACHER: What number comes after 4? ☐ What number comes before 7? ☐

Numbers 1-10 and Math Stories: Park Scene

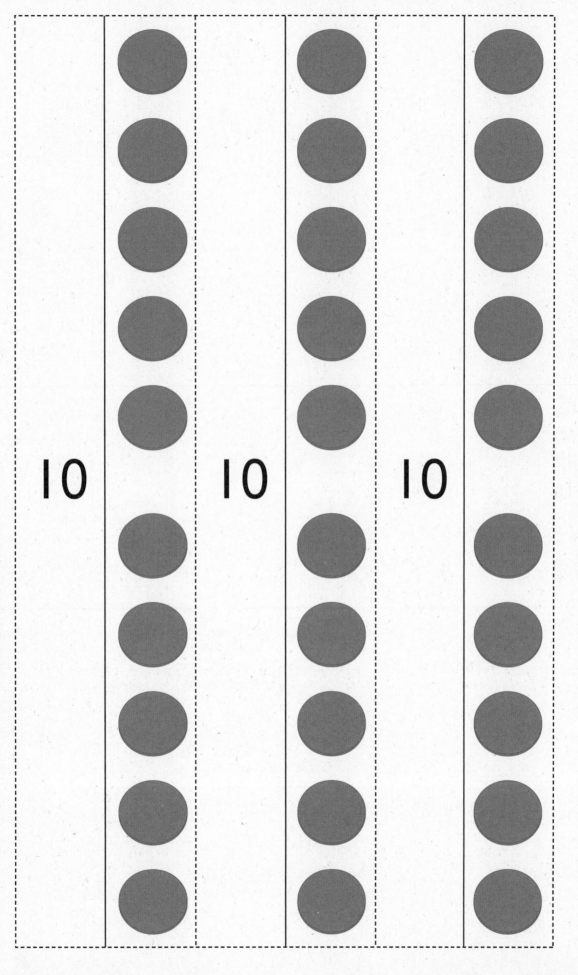

Cut on dashed lines. Fold on solid lines and tape at top and bottom.

10   10   10

© Houghton Mifflin Harcourt Publishing Company

10-Counter Strips

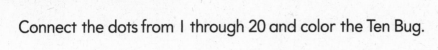

Name _____

Connect the dots from 1 through 20 and color the Ten Bug.

9
8
7
6
5
4
3
2
1

10
11
12
13
14
15
16
17
18
19
20

Ring a group of 10 in each box. Count and color the items. Use the colors shown.

11—red 13—orange
12—blue 14—green

 Check Understanding

TEACHER: Explain how ringing a group of 10 helps you count.

Dear Family:

Your child is learning about partners of numbers. We call the number pairs that make up a number "partners" because they go together to make that number. For example,

6 has partners: 1 and 5   2 and 4   3 and 3

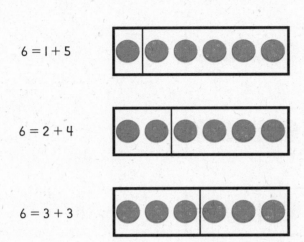

$6 = 1 + 5$

$6 = 2 + 4$

$6 = 3 + 3$

The partner idea is very important for understanding numbers. It will help your child understand addition and subtraction. You can help your child see partners in everyday life. When you have a small number of objects, for example, 5 crackers, you can ask your child to make the partners of 5. Your child can show 1 and 4 crackers and can also show 2 and 3 crackers. Doing this often with different objects will help your child understand numbers.

Thank you!

Sincerely,
Your child's teacher

CC SS Unit 3 addresses the following standards from the Common Core State Standards for Mathematics: **K.CC.A.1, K.CC.A.2, K.CC.A.3, K.CC.B.4, K.CC.B.4.a, K.CC.B.4.b, K.CC.B.4.c, K.CC.B.5, K.CC.C.6, K.CC.C.7, K.OA.A.1, K.OA.A.2, K.OA.A.3, K.OA.A.5, K.NBT.A.1, K.MD.B.3, K.G.A.1, K.G.A.2, K.G.B.4, K.G.B.5, K.G.B.6,** and all Mathematical Practices.

Estimada familia:

Su niño está aprendiendo sobre las partes de los números. Llamamos "partes" a los pares de números que pueden juntarse para formar un determinado número. Por ejemplo,

6 tiene las partes: 1 y 5   2 y 4   3 y 3

6 = 1 + 5

6 = 2 + 4

6 = 3 + 3

La idea de las partes es muy importante para entender los números. Ayudará a su niño a entender la suma y la resta. Ud. puede ayudar a su niño a ver partes en la vida diaria. Cuando tenga un pequeño número de objetos, por ejemplo 5 galletas, puede pedirle a su niño que muestre las partes de 5. Su niño puede mostrar 1 galleta y 4 galletas y también 2 galletas y 3 galletas. Hacer esto a menudo con distintos objetos puede ayudar a su niño a entender los números.

¡Gracias!

Atentamente,
El maestro de su niño

© Houghton Mifflin Harcourt Publishing Company

Name _____

 Write the 4 partners.

$$4 = \boxed{} + \boxed{}$$

$$4 = \boxed{} + \boxed{}$$

 Write the 5 partners.

$$5 = \boxed{} + \boxed{}$$

$$5 = \boxed{} + \boxed{}$$

$$5 = \boxed{} + \boxed{}$$

$$5 = \boxed{} + \boxed{}$$

Write the 6 partners.

7

$6 = \boxed{} + \boxed{}$

8

$6 = \boxed{} + \boxed{}$

9

$6 = \boxed{} + \boxed{}$

10

$6 = \boxed{} + \boxed{}$

11

$6 = \boxed{} + \boxed{}$

✓ **Check Understanding**
TEACHER: Explain why there are no switched partners for $6 = 3 + 3$.

Explore Partners Through 6

Name _____

Count how many. Write the number.

1

2

3

4

5 Write the numbers 1–10.

6 PATH to FLUENCY **Add** the numbers.

$0 + 3 =$ ☐ $2 + 0 =$ ☐ $4 + 0 =$ ☐

$2 + 1 =$ ☐ $1 + 4 =$ ☐ $1 + 1 =$ ☐

$0 + 2 =$ ☐ $1 + 2 =$ ☐ $2 + 2 =$ ☐

$0 + 3 =$ ☐ $3 + 1 =$ ☐ $2 + 3 =$ ☐

$4 + 1 =$ ☐ $5 + 0 =$ ☐ $1 + 4 =$ ☐

7 PATH to FLUENCY **Subtract** the numbers.

$3 - 0 =$ ☐ $2 - 0 =$ ☐ $4 - 0 =$ ☐

$4 - 1 =$ ☐ $5 - 1 =$ ☐ $1 - 1 =$ ☐

$5 - 2 =$ ☐ $4 - 2 =$ ☐ $3 - 2 =$ ☐

$3 - 3 =$ ☐ $5 - 3 =$ ☐ $4 - 3 =$ ☐

✔ **Check Understanding**
TEACHER: Explain what the + sign and – sign mean.

Addition and Subtraction Stories: Park Scene

Dear Family:

When children first start counting, they count objects one at a time. Helping children see 5-groups and 10-groups enables them to understand larger (greater) numbers. We are learning that if we can see groups of objects as 5-groups and 10-groups, then we can understand greater numbers. Children learn to make these groups with objects. Later, they will see them as organized groups in their minds.

Your child is learning that the teen numbers 11, 12, 13, 14, 15, 16, 17, 18, and 19 each have a 10 inside: $11 = 10 + 1$, $12 = 10 + 2$, and so on through $19 = 10 + 9$.

Have your child practice counting groups of objects. Your child can find and separate the 10-group from the total quantity to see the 10 hiding inside the teen number.

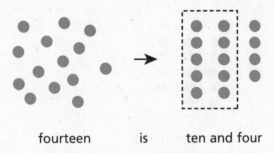

fourteen   is   ten and four

Your child can then show this number by using the number cards.

Thank you for your cooperation!

Sincerely,
Your child's teacher

© Houghton Mifflin Harcourt Publishing Company

Estimada familia:

Cuando los niños empiezan a contar, suelen contar los objetos uno por uno. Ayudarlos a ver los objetos en grupos de 5 y grupos de 10, les facilita el aprendizaje de números más grandes (mayores). Estamos aprendiendo que si podemos ver grupos de objetos como grupos de 5 y grupos de 10, entonces podemos entender números más grandes. Los niños aprenden a formar estos grupos con objetos. Más adelante, los verán mentalmente como grupos organizados.

Su niño está aprendiendo que los números 11, 12, 13, 14, 15, 16, 17, 18 y 19 contienen 10: 11 = 10 + 1, 12 = 10 + 2, y así sucesivamente, hasta 19 = 10 + 9.

Pida a su niño que practique contando grupos de objetos. Su niño puede separar el grupo de 10 de la cantidad total, para ver el 10 escondido en los números de 11 a 19.

catorce   es   diez más cuatro

Después, su niño puede mostrar este número usando las tarjetas de números.

¡Gracias por su colaboración!

Atentamente,
El maestro de su niño

CC SS En la Unidad 3 se aplican los siguientes estándares de los Estándares estatales comunes de matemáticas: **K.CC.A.1, K.CC.A.2, K.CC.A.3, K.CC.B.4, K.CC.B.4.a, K.CC.B.4.b, K.CC.B.4.c, K.CC.B.5, K.CC.C.6, K.CC.C.7, K.OA.A.1, K.OA.A.2, K.OA.A.3, K.OA.A.5, K.NBT.A.1, K.MD.B.3, K.G.A.1, K.G.A.2, K.G.B.4, K.G.B.5, K.G.B.6 y todos los de** Prácticas matemáticas.

1

2

3

4

5

6

7

8

9

10

1

2

3

4

5

6

7

8

9

0

At Home Number Cards

Name _____

1 Draw the circles on the Number Parade. Use a 5-group.

6	7	8	9	10

---

2 Use the 5-group. Draw to show the number.

9 = ⬚

6 = ⬚

8 = ⬚

10 = ⬚

7 = ⬚

3 Write the number.

☐ = [○○○○○ / ○○○]

☐ = [○○○○○]

☐ = [○○○○]

☐ = [○○○○○ / ○]

☐ = [○○]

☐ = [○○○○○ / ○○○]

☐ = [○○○○○ / ○○○○]

☐ = [○○○○○ / ○○○]

☐ = [○○○○○ / ○○]

☐ = [○○○○○ / ○]

☐ = [○○○○○ / ○○]

☐ = [○○○]

④ Write the number 11.

⑤ Write the number 12.

⑥ (PATH to FLUENCY) Add the numbers.

$2 + 0 = \boxed{}$ $0 + 3 = \boxed{}$ $5 + 0 = \boxed{}$

$2 + 2 = \boxed{}$ $1 + 2 = \boxed{}$ $2 + 3 = \boxed{}$

⑦ (PATH to FLUENCY) Subtract the numbers.

$4 - 0 = \boxed{}$ $2 - 1 = \boxed{}$ $3 - 1 = \boxed{}$

$4 - 2 = \boxed{}$ $5 - 2 = \boxed{}$ $5 - 3 = \boxed{}$

 Check Understanding

TEACHER: Draw 10 objects using 5-groups.

More Groups of 10

Dear Family:

When children first learn to write numbers, emphasis is placed on forming the numbers correctly. Children begin by tracing, and then are provided with starting points for their pencils. Learning the correct technique helps children learn to write numbers neatly and consistently.

After awhile, children no longer need these hints and are able to write without guide lines or starting points. It is easier for many children to write smaller figures, since they have greater control of the writing tool. With practice, children will gain confidence and speed in writing numbers.

In Unit 3, children continue to practice writing numbers, including 2-digit numbers from 11 to 20. They are already familiar with the individual numbers they will be using. When writing 2-digit numbers, children learn the proper placement and spacing between numbers. The numbers should not be too close together or too far apart, but just the right distance to be read and understood.

Please help and encourage your child as he or she learns to write numbers. This will take time and practice.

Thank you!

Sincerely,
Your child's teacher

CC SS Unit 3 addresses the following standards from the Common Core State Standards for Mathematics: **K.CC.A.1, K.CC.A.2, K.CC.A.3, K.CC.B.4, K.CC.B.4.a, K.CC.B.4.b, K.CC.B.4.c, K.CC.B.5, K.CC.C.6, K.CC.C.7, K.OA.A.1, K.OA.A.2, K.OA.A.3, K.OA.A.5, K.NBT.A.1, K.MD.B.3, K.G.A.1, K.G.A.2, K.G.B.4, K.G.B.5, K.G.B.6,** and all Mathematical Practices.

Estimada familia:

Cuando los niños aprenden a escribir los números, se enfatiza que deben trazarlos correctamente. Se comienza calcando y luego, se les proporcionan puntos desde donde deben comenzar con sus lápices. Aprender la técnica exacta les servirá a los niños para escribir consistentemente los números de manera correcta.

Después de un tiempo, ya no necesitan estas pistas y pueden escribir sin líneas que les guíen y sin puntos donde comenzar. Es más fácil para muchos niños trazar números pequeños, ya que así tienen más control del instrumento de escritura. Con práctica, los niños adquirirán confianza y velocidad para escribir los números.

En la Unidad 3, los niños continúan practicando la escritura de números, incluyendo los números de 2 dígitos del 11 al 20. Ya están familiarizados con los números individuales que estarán usando. Al escribir números de 2 dígitos, deben aprender su colocación correcta y la distancia correcta que debe haber entre los dígitos. No deben estar demasiado juntos ni demasiado separados, la distancia debe ser adecuada para poder leerlos y comprenderlos.

Por favor ayude a su niño a escribir los números. Esto requerirá tiempo y práctica. Anímelo y apóyelo durante el aprendizaje.

¡Gracias!

Atentamente,
El maestro de su niño

CCSS **En la Unidad 3 se aplican los siguientes estándares de los** Estándares estatales comunes de matemáticas: **K.CC.A.1, K.CC.A.2, K.CC.A.3, K.CC.B.4, K.CC.B.4.a, K.CC.B.4.b, K.CC.B.4.c, K.CC.B.5, K.CC.C.6, K.CC.C.7, K.OA.A.1, K.OA.A.2, K.OA.A.3, K.OA.A.5, K.NBT.A.1, K.MD.B.3, K.G.A.1, K.G.A.2, K.G.B.4, K.G.B.5, K.G.B.6, y todos los de** Prácticas matemáticas.

Name _____

1 Write the number 13.

13 13 13 13 13 13

13

13

13

13

2 Write the number 14.

14 14 14 14 14 14

14

14

14

14

© Houghton Mifflin Harcourt Publishing Company

3 PATH to FLUENCY Add the numbers.

$0 + 2 = \square$	$1 + 0 = \square$	$0 + 5 = \square$
$3 + 1 = \square$	$1 + 3 = \square$	$0 + 1 = \square$
$2 + 3 = \square$	$2 + 1 = \square$	$3 + 2 = \square$
$0 + 4 = \square$	$4 + 1 = \square$	$5 + 0 = \square$

4 PATH to FLUENCY Subtract the numbers.

$1 - 0 = \square$	$4 - 0 = \square$	$2 - 0 = \square$
$5 - 1 = \square$	$3 - 1 = \square$	$4 - 1 = \square$
$5 - 3 = \square$	$4 - 3 = \square$	$3 - 3 = \square$
$4 - 4 = \square$	$5 - 5 = \square$	$5 - 4 = \square$

✓ **Check Understanding**

TEACHER: Draw 4 dots and a Break-Apart Stick. Then write a matching equation below.

Model Partners Through 6 with Counters

Name _____

1 Draw the circles on the Number Parade. Use a 5-group.

6	7	8	9	10

2 Use the 5-group. Draw to show the number.

6 = ⬜ ○○○○○

7 = ⬜ ○○○○○

8 = ⬜ ○○○○○

9 = ⬜ ○○○○○

10 = ⬜ ○○○○○

3 Write the number.

⬜ = ○○○

⬜ = ○○○○○ / ○○○○

⬜ = ○○

⬜ = ○○○○ / ○○○

⬜ = ○○○○○ / ○

⬜ = ○○○○○ / ○○○

⬜ = ○○○○○ / ○○

⬜ = ○○○○

⬜ = ○○○○○ / ○○○○

⬜ = ○○○○

⬜ = ○○○○○ / ○○○○

⬜ = ○○○○

④ Write the number 15.

15 15 15 15 15 15

15

⑤ Write the number 16.

16 16 16 16 16 16

16

⑥ **PATH to FLUENCY** Add the numbers.

5 + 0 = ☐   0 + 3 = ☐   4 + 0 = ☐

2 + 2 = ☐   3 + 2 = ☐   1 + 4 = ☐

⑦ **PATH to FLUENCY** Subtract the numbers.

3 − 0 = ☐   1 − 0 = ☐   2 − 0 = ☐

2 − 1 = ☐   5 − 1 = ☐   3 − 1 = ☐

5 − 2 = ☐   5 − 4 = ☐   4 − 2 = ☐

✓ **Check Understanding**
TEACHER: Draw a picture to show 2 + 3.

© Houghton Mifflin Harcourt Publishing Company

More Addition and Subtraction Stories: Park Scene

Name _____

Use a 10-group.

Write the partners.

1

11 = ☐ + ☐

2

12 = ☐ + ☐

3

13 = ☐ + ☐

4

14 = ☐ + ☐

Content Standards **K.CC.A.3, K.CC.B.4.b, K.CC.B.5, K.OA.A.1, K.NBT.A.1**
Mathematical Practices **MP7**

Show Tens and Ones **145**

Use a 10-group.

Write the partners.

5

$$15 = \boxed{} + \boxed{}$$

6

$$16 = \boxed{} + \boxed{}$$

7

$$17 = \boxed{} + \boxed{}$$

 Check Understanding

TEACHER: Draw 5-Square Tiles and Square-Inch Tiles to show the number.

18

Show Tens and Ones

Name _____

Build the shape.

1

2

3

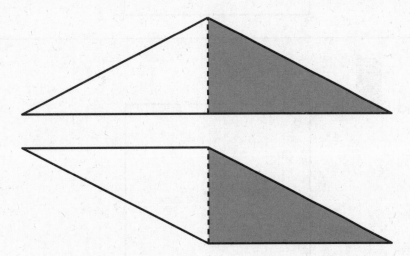

Build. Trace the shapes. Color.

4 Use 4 .

5 Use 4 .

6 Use 1 and 1 .

Make New Shapes

Name _____

Build. Trace the shapes. Color.

© Houghton Mifflin Harcourt Publishing Company

Build. Trace the shapes. Color.

Build a shape. Trace the outline of the shape.

⑬

✓ **Check Understanding**

TEACHER: Ring the shapes you could use to make this shape.

Make New Shapes

Sorting Cards

Name _____

1 Color the circles red.

2 Color the squares blue.

3 Color the triangles green.

4 Color the rectangles purple.

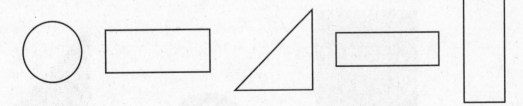

5 Color all the shapes with 4 sides orange.

CC SS Content Standards **K.MD.B.3, K.G.A.2, K.G.B.4**
Mathematical Practices **MP2, MP3**

Explore Classifying **153**

Ring the squares.

Draw a line under the green shapes.

✔ Check Understanding

TEACHER: Name three different ways objects can be sorted.

Explore Classifying

Sorting Cards

Name _____

1 Draw circles for 1–10.
Show the 5-groups.

1	
2	
3	
4	
5	
6	
7	
8	
9	
10	

2 Use the 5-group. Draw to show the number.

9 = ⬜(○○○○)

7 = ⬜(○○○○)

8 = ⬜(○○○○)

10 = ⬜(○○○○)

6 = ⬜(○○○○)

9 = ⬜(○○○○○)

7 = ⬜(○○○○○)

8 = ⬜(○○○○)

3 Count how many. Write the number.

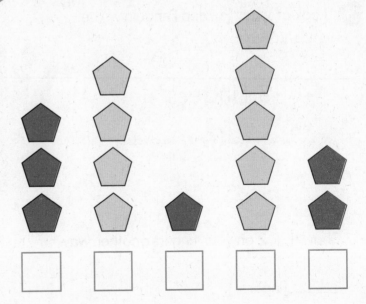

© Houghton Mifflin Harcourt Publishing Company

Content Standards **K.CC.A.2, K.CC.A.3, K.CC.B.4,
K.CC.B.4.b, K.CC.B.4.c, K.CC.B.5, K.OA.A.1**
Mathematical Practices **MP3, MP6, MP7**

Practice Addition and Subtraction Stories: Park Scene   157

Help Puzzled Penguin.

4 Look at Puzzled Penguin's answers.

⬚⬚⬚⬚⬚ ⬚ = 6

⬚⬚⬚⬚⬚ ⬚⬚⬚ = 9

⬚⬚⬚⬚⬚ ⬚⬚ = 7

⬚⬚⬚⬚⬚ ⬚⬚⬚⬚ = 8

Am I correct?

5 Look at what Puzzled Penguin wrote.

8 fingers

Show 4 + 2 on your fingers another way.

_____ fingers

 Check Understanding
TEACHER: Tell a story that has a total of 9. Draw a picture to match.

Practice Addition and Subtraction Stories: Park Scene

© Houghton Mifflin Harcourt Publishing Company

Sorting Cards

Sorting Cards

Name _____

1 Draw circles for 1–10. Show the 5-group.

1	2	3	4	5	6	7	8	9	10
								○○○○○○○○○	

2 Write each number and an **equal to sign (=)** or a **not equal to sign (≠)**.

2	≠	4				

CC SS Content Standards **K.CC.A.3, K.CC.B.4.c, K.CC.C.7, K.OA.A.5, K.MD.B.3**
Mathematical Practices **MP2**

3 PATH to FLUENCY **Add the numbers.**

0 + 4 = ☐   0 + 0 = ☐   4 + 1 = ☐

2 + 2 = ☐   2 + 0 = ☐   0 + 2 = ☐

2 + 3 = ☐   1 + 4 = ☐   3 + 2 = ☐

4 PATH to FLUENCY **Subtract the numbers.**

0 − 0 = ☐   1 − 0 = ☐   4 − 0 = ☐

5 − 2 = ☐   3 − 2 = ☐   2 − 1 = ☐

4 − 3 = ☐   5 − 3 = ☐   3 − 3 = ☐

3 − 1 = ☐   4 − 1 = ☐   2 − 2 = ☐

✓ Check Understanding

TEACHER: How are these shapes sorted? _____

Practice Classifying

1 Write the number. Draw it using the 5-group.

= ☐

○○○○○

= ☐

○○○○○

= ☐

○○○○○

= ☐

○○○○○

2 Use the 5-group. Draw to show the number.

7 = | ○○○○○ |

10 = | ○○○○○ |

9 = | ○○○○○ |

7 = | ○○○○○ |

6 = | ○○○○○ |

9 = | ○○○○○ |

8 = | ○○○○○ |

6 = | ○○○○○ |

3 Write the number.

| ○○○○○ ○○ | = ☐

| ○○○○○ ○○ | = ☐

| ○○○○ | = ☐

| ○○○○○ ○○○ | = ☐

| ○○○○○ ○○○ | = ☐

| ○○○○○ | = ☐

| ○○○○○ ○ | = ☐

| ○○○○○ ○○○○ | = ☐

4 Draw a ring around every 5-group.
Write the numbers shown by the circles.

5 Look at what Puzzled Penguin drew.
Help Puzzled Penguin.

Am I correct?

1	2	3	4	5	6	7	8	9	10

✓ Check Understanding

TEACHER: Explain why you can use two 5-Square Tiles instead of 10 Square-Inch Tiles to show a group of 10.

© Houghton Mifflin Harcourt Publishing Company

Build Teen Numbers

Name _____

1 Draw circles for 1–10. Show the 5-group.

1	2	3	4	5	6	7	8	9	10
							○○○○○○○○		

2 Write each number and an equal to sign (=) or a not equal to sign (≠).

5	=	5

☐   ☐

☐   ☐

☐   ☐

☐   ☐

☐   ☐

CC SS Content Standards K.CC.A.3, K.CC.B.4, K.CC.B.4.c, K.CC.B.5, K.CC.C.7, K.OA.A.5
Mathematical Practices MP2, MP3, MP6, MP8

Practice with 5-Groups **167**

3 Write the number 15.

4 Write the number 16.

5 **PATH to FLUENCY** Add the numbers.

$0 + 2 = \boxed{}$ $3 + 2 = \boxed{}$ $0 + 4 = \boxed{}$

6 **PATH to FLUENCY** Subtract the numbers.

$5 - 2 = \boxed{}$ $5 - 4 = \boxed{}$ $4 - 2 = \boxed{}$

✓ **Check Understanding**

TEACHER: Draw 2 groups of objects correctly using the not equal to sign (≠) between them. Then repeat with 2 groups with the equal to sign (=).

Practice with 5-Groups

15

10 + 5

14

10 + 4

10 + 9

13

10 + 3

19

10 + 8

12

10 + 2

18

10 + 7

11

10 + 1

17

16

10 + 6

Teen Total Cards

Name _____

VOCABULARY
teen number

Use a 10-group.
Write the partners.
Write the **teen number**.

1

☐ + ☐ = ☐

2

☐ + ☐ = ☐

3

☐ + ☐ = ☐

4

☐ + ☐ = ☐

5

☐ + ☐ = ☐

6

☐ + ☐ = ☐

7

☐ + ☐ = ☐

8

☐ + ☐ = ☐

© Houghton Mifflin Harcourt Publishing Company

Content Standards K.CC.A.2, K.CC.A.3, K.CC.B.4, K.CC.B.5, K.OA.A.1, K.NBT.A.1 **Mathematical Practices** MP6

Tens in Teens 171

Use a 10-group.

Write the teen number.

9

10

11

12

13

14

✔ Check Understanding

TEACHER: Draw a 10-group and some extras to show 13.

© Houghton Mifflin Harcourt Publishing Company

Tens in Teens

Name _____

Find partners for 6.

Draw squares to show the **unknown** partner.

Write the partners.

1

 |

□   □

2

 |

□   □

3

 |

□   □

Find partners for 7.

Draw squares to show the unknown partner.

Write the partners.

4

☐   ☐

5

☐   ☐

6

☐   ☐

© Houghton Mifflin Harcourt Publishing Company

✔ **Check Understanding**

TEACHER: Draw two more partners for 7 that are not shown on this page.

       Stories and Partners

Write the partners.

2

☐ + ☐

3

☐ + ☐

3

☐ + ☐

4

☐ + ☐

4

☐ + ☐

4

☐ + ☐

5

☐ + ☐

5

☐ + ☐

5

☐ + ☐

5

☐ + ☐

Write the partners.

6

☐ + ☐

6

☐ + ☐

6

☐ + ☐

6

☐ + ☐

6

☐ + ☐

7

☐ + ☐

7

☐ + ☐

7

☐ + ☐

7

☐ + ☐

7

☐ + ☐

7

☐ + ☐

✓ Check Understanding

TEACHER: Write the unknown partners.

5
 ☐ +2

6
4+ ☐

7
☐ +1

Practice with Partners

© Houghton Mifflin Harcourt Publishing Company

Dear Family:

In the next few days, please find 20 of the same kind of small object that your child can take to school and paste onto a sheet of paper. For example, your child can use buttons or stickers, or you can cut out 20 small pieces of paper or fabric.

The objects will be used for an activity to help your child learn to see the group of 10 inside each of the teen numbers: 11, 12, 13, 14, 15, 16, 17, 18, and 19.

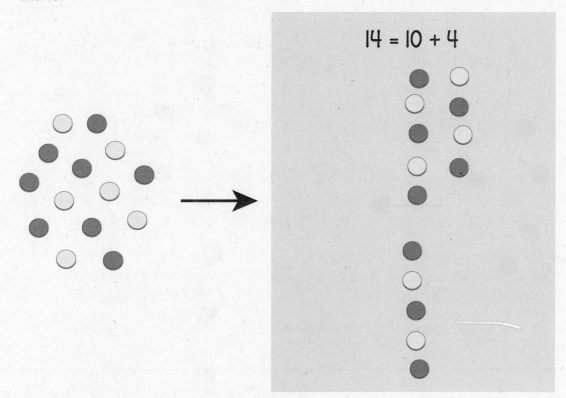

Thank you for your cooperation!

Sincerely,
Your child's teacher

CC SS Unit 3 addresses the following standards from the Common Core State Standards for Mathematics: **K.CC.A.1, K.CC.A.2, K.CC.A.3, K.CC.B.4, K.CC.B.4.a, K.CC.B.4.b, K.CC.B.4.c, K.CC.B.5, K.CC.C.6, K.CC.C.7, K.OA.A.1, K.OA.A.2, K.OA.A.3, K.OA.A.5, K.NBT.A.1, K.MD.B.3, K.G.A.1, K.G.A.2, K.G.B.4, K.G.B.5, K.G.B.6,** and all Mathematical Practices.

Estimada familia:

Durante los días siguientes, por favor busque 20 objetos pequeños, del mismo tipo, que su niño pueda llevar a la escuela y pegar en una hoja de papel. Por ejemplo, su niño puede usar botones o adhesivos, o usted puede cortar 20 pedacitos de papel o tela.

Los objetos se usarán en una actividad que ayudará a su niño a identificar el grupo de 10 que hay en cada uno de los números de 11 a 19: 11, 12, 13, 14, 15, 16, 17, 18 y 19.

¡Gracias por su colaboración!

Atentamente,
El maestro de su niño

En la Unidad 3 se aplican los siguientes estándares de los Estándares estatales comunes de matemáticas: K.CC.A.1, K.CC.A.2, K.CC.A.3, K.CC.B.4, K.CC.B.4.a, K.CC.B.4.b, K.CC.B.4.c, K.CC.B.5, K.CC.C.6, K.CC.C.7, K.OA.A.1, K.OA.A.2, K.OA.A.3, K.OA.A.5, K.NBT.A.1, K.MD.B.3, K.G.A.1, K.G.A.2, K.G.B.4, K.G.B.5, K.G.B.6 y todos los de Prácticas matemáticas.

Build Teen Numbers with Classroom Objects

Name _____

1 Write the partners. Look for switched partners.

5

☐ + ☐

5

☐ + ☐

5

☐ + ☐

6

☐ + ☐

6

☐ + ☐

6

☐ + ☐

7

☐ + ☐

7

☐ + ☐

7

☐ + ☐

5

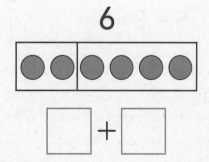

☐ + ☐

6

☐ + ☐

7

☐ + ☐

CC SS **Content Standards K.CC.A.3, K.OA.A.3, K.OA.A.5**
Mathematical Practices MP8

2 Write the number 17.

17 17 17 17 17 17

17 17 17 17 17 17

3 Write the number 18.

18 18 18 18 18 18

18 18 18 18 18 18

4 PATH to FLUENCY Add the numbers.

$1 + 0 = \boxed{}$ $1 + 3 = \boxed{}$ $4 + 1 = \boxed{}$

$3 + 2 = \boxed{}$ $2 + 2 = \boxed{}$ $2 + 3 = \boxed{}$

5 PATH to FLUENCY Subtract the numbers.

$3 - 0 = \boxed{}$ $5 - 1 = \boxed{}$ $5 - 0 = \boxed{}$

$5 - 2 = \boxed{}$ $5 - 3 = \boxed{}$ $4 - 3 = \boxed{}$

✓ **Check Understanding**

TEACHER: Draw objects to show all the partners for 5 including the switched partners.

Build Teen Numbers with Classroom Objects

1 Puzzled Penguin showed the partners
for two teen numbers and wrote the total.
Help Puzzled Penguin.

$\underline{12} = 10 + 3$ $\underline{13} = 10 + 2$

Am I correct?

2 Draw the buttons. Write the total.

$\underline{} = 10 + 5$ $\underline{} = 10 + 1$

3 Write the number 19.

19   19   19   19   19

19

4 Write the number 20.

20   20   20   20   20

20

5 PATH to FLUENCY **Add the numbers.**

$2 + 0 = \boxed{}$ $0 + 2 = \boxed{}$ $4 + 0 = \boxed{}$

$1 + 4 = \boxed{}$ $5 + 0 = \boxed{}$ $2 + 3 = \boxed{}$

6 PATH to FLUENCY **Subtract the numbers.**

$4 - 1 = \boxed{}$ $4 - 0 = \boxed{}$ $2 - 1 = \boxed{}$

$4 - 2 = \boxed{}$ $1 - 1 = \boxed{}$ $3 - 2 = \boxed{}$

✓ **Check Understanding**

TEACHER: Use some counters. Show 3 different ways to arrange them.

   Show Teen Numbers with Classroom Objects

Name _____

Write the partners for each teen number.

1 12 = [ ] + [ ]

2 14 = [ ] + [ ]

3 13 = [ ] + [ ]

4 16 = [ ] + [ ]

5 18 = [ ] + [ ]

6 19 = [ ] + [ ]

Content Standards K.CC.A.3, K.CC.B.4, K.CC.B.5, K.OA.A.1, K.NBT.A.1
Mathematical Practices MP6

Look at the total and partners.

Draw buttons to match.

7 $11 = 10 + 1$

8 $16 = 10 + 6$

9 $15 = 10 + 5$

10 $17 = 10 + 7$

✔ **Check Understanding**

TEACHER: Write the unknown partners.

$16 = 10 +$ ☐

$18 = 10 +$ ☐

Object Collections: Teen Numbers

Name _____

Color all the shapes of one kind the color shown below.

Count the number of each shape in the picture. Write the number.

Draw your own smiling faces!

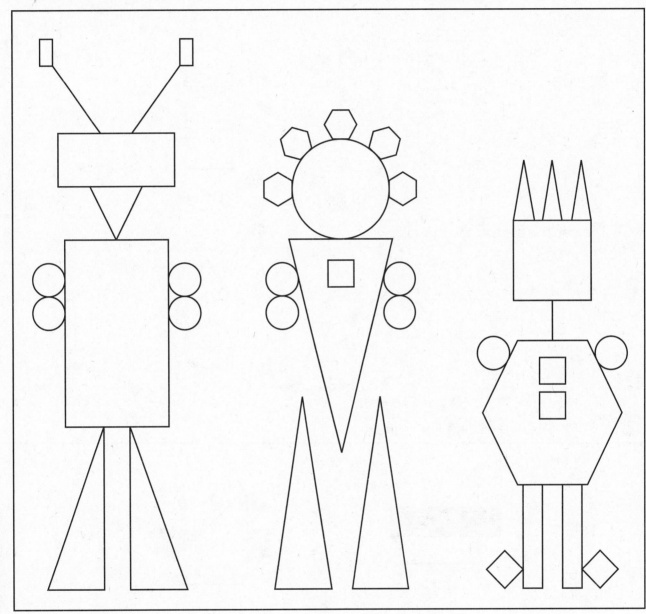

square	rectangle	circle	triangle	hexagon

CC SS Content Standards **K.CC.B.5, K.G.A.1, K.G.A.2**
Mathematical Practices **MP3, MP6, MP7**

Focus on Mathematical Practices **185**

Ring the picture that matches the statement.

VOCABULARY
below
beside
behind
next to

1 The hexagon is **below** the square.

2 The circle is **beside** the triangle.

3 The rectangle is **behind** the triangle.

4 The circle is **next to** the square.

Focus on Mathematical Practices

Write the partners.

1

6

☐ + ☐

2

6

☐ + ☐

3 Ring a group of 10. Count all of the stars.
Write how many in all.

4 Ring the number. Draw it using the 5-group.

| 6 |
| 7 |
| 8 |

○○○○○

5 Write each number. Ring = or ≠.

	=	
	≠	

6 Choose all the partners that are equal to 6.

○

○

○

7 Add the numbers. Ring the answer.

3 + 1 = ☐

2	3	4

8 Subtract the numbers. Ring the answer.

4 − 2 = ☐

2	3	4

Use the picture below to complete Exercises 9–12.

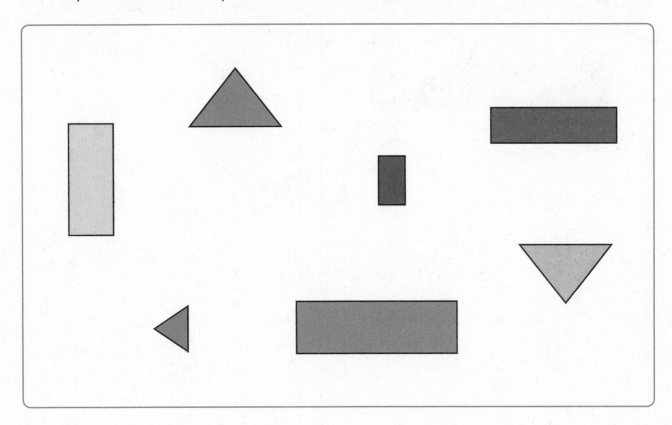

9 Ring all of the shapes with 4 sides.

10 How many triangles are there?
○ 2   ○ 3   ○ 4

11 How many rectangles are there?
○ 2   ○ 3   ○ 4

12 Are there more triangles or rectangles? Ring the shape.

13 Two triangles are joined. Draw a shape they could make.

14 Draw a triangle. Draw a circle below it.

15 Draw to show the story problem. Write the answer.
Shane sees 5 butterflies. Tony sees 2 butterflies.
How many butterflies do they see in all?

butterflies

Favorite Places

Part A

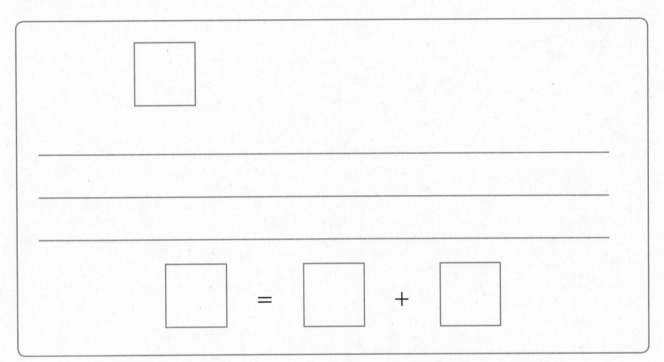

Name _____

Part B

A

above

The bird is **above** the tree.

add

$$3 + 2 = 5$$

B

behind

The boy is **behind** the fence.

below

The tree is **below** the bird.

beside

The slide is **beside** the tree.

C

capacity

Capacity is the amount a container can hold.

Glossary

circle

classify

apples

not apples

column

1	11	21	31	41	51	61	71	81	91
2	12	22	32	42	52	62	72	82	92
3	13	23	33	43	53	63	73	83	93
4	14	24	34	44	54	64	74	84	94
5	15	25	35	45	55	65	75	85	95
6	16	26	36	46	56	66	76	86	96
7	17	27	37	47	57	67	77	87	97
8	18	28	38	48	58	68	78	88	98
9	19	29	39	49	59	69	79	89	99
10	20	30	40	50	60	70	80	90	100

cone

corner

corner

count

cube

cylinder

D

decade numbers

10, 20, 30, 40, 50, 60, 70, 80, 90

E

eight

8

equal to sign (=)

4 + 4 = 8

4 plus 4 is **equal to** 8.

equation

Examples:

4 + 3 = 7   7 = 4 + 3

9 − 5 = 4   4 = 9 − 5

F

face

face

fewer

There are **fewer** blue tiles than red tiles.

five

5

flat shapes

four

4

G

greater

3   5

greater

Glossary

greater than

9 is **greater than** 6.

group

This **group** has 3 circles.

H

heavier

heavier

height

Height is how tall a person or an object is.

hexagon

how many

Example:

How many fingers? 5 fingers

© Houghton Mifflin Harcourt Publishing Company

S4 Glossary

I

in front of

The girl is **in front of** the fence.

L

larger

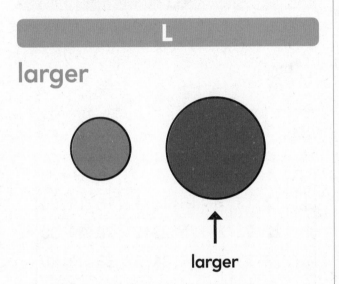

larger

left

The yellow square is on the **left.**

length

The **length** of this pencil is 6 paper clips.

less

3   5

↑
less

less than

9

11

9 is **less than** 11.

lighter

lighter

longer

longer

The pencil is **longer** than the crayon.

M

minus (–)

8 – 3 = 5

8 **minus** 3 equals 5.

more

There are **more** red tiles than blue tiles.

N

next to

The tree is **next to** the slide.

nine

9 [nine cubes]

not equal to sign (≠)

6 ≠ 8

6 is **not equal to** 8.

O

one

1 [one cube]

one hundred

1	2	3	4	5	6	7	8	9	10
11	12	13	14	15	16	17	18	19	20
21	22	23	24	25	26	27	28	29	30
31	32	33	34	35	36	37	38	39	40
41	42	43	44	45	46	47	48	49	50
51	52	53	54	55	56	57	58	59	60
61	62	63	64	65	66	67	68	69	70
71	72	73	74	75	76	77	78	79	80
81	82	83	84	85	86	87	88	89	90
91	92	93	94	95	96	97	98	99	100

ones

18 has 8 **ones**.

order

1	2	3	4	5	6	7	8	9	10

These numbers are in **order**.

P

plus (+)

3 + 2 = 5

3 **plus** 2 equals 5.

R

rectangle

A square is a special kind of rectangle.

right

The green square is on the **right**.

roll

row

1	11	21	31	41	51	61	71	81	91
2	12	22	32	42	52	62	72	82	92
3	13	23	33	43	53	63	73	83	93
4	14	24	34	44	54	64	74	84	94
5	15	25	35	45	55	65	75	85	95
6	16	26	36	46	56	66	76	86	96
7	17	27	37	47	57	67	77	87	97
8	18	28	38	48	58	68	78	88	98
9	19	29	39	49	59	69	79	89	99
10	20	30	40	50	60	70	80	90	100

S

seven

7

Glossary

shorter (height)

shorter

The yellow flower is **shorter** than the red flower.

shorter (length)

shorter

The crayon is **shorter** than the pencil.

side

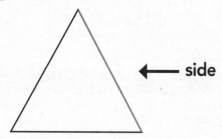

← **side**

six

6

smaller

smaller

solid shapes

sort

You can **sort** animals into groups.

sphere

square

stack

story problem

Example:

There are 2 bunnies in the garden.
Then 3 more bunnies come.
How many bunnies are there in total?

straight lines

Straight lines do not curve.

subtract

$8 - 3 = 5$

●●●●● ●●●

| T |

taller

taller

The red flower is **taller** than the
yellow flower.

teen numbers

11 12 13 14 15 16 17 18 19

Glossary

ten
10

three
3

three-dimensional shapes

total
$$4 + 3 = 7$$
total

triangle

two
2

two-dimensional shapes

U
unknown
$$3 + 4 = \square \qquad 3 + \square = 7$$
unknown

W
weight
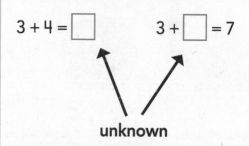

Weight is how heavy an object is.

Z
zero
0

There are **zero** apples on the plate.

Common Core State Standards for Mathematical Content

K.CC Counting and Cardinality

Know number names and the count sequence.

K.CC.A.1	Count to 100 by ones and by tens.	Unit 1 Lessons 1, 2, 3, 4, 5, 7, 11, 17; Unit 2 Lessons 6, 8, 10, 18, 19; Unit 3 Lessons 1, 2; Unit 4 Lessons 12, 15, 16, 17; Unit 5 Lessons 2, 3, 5, 8, 10, 13, 23
K.CC.A.2	Count forward beginning from a given number within the known sequence (instead of having to begin at 1).	Unit 2 Lessons 1, 9, 10, 14, 18, 19; Unit 3 Lessons 5, 7, 11, 13, 15; Unit 4 Lessons 3, 5, 7, 12, 15, 16, 17, 18, 20; Unit 5 Lessons 3, 4, 5, 7, 8, 9, 10, 15, 18, 19
K.CC.A.3	Write numbers from 0 to 20. Represent a number of objects with a written numeral 0–20 (with 0 representing a count of no objects).	Unit 1 Lessons 6, 12, 13, 14, 16, 17; Unit 2 Lessons 1, 5, 7, 8, 9, 10, 11, 15, 18, 19, 20; Unit 3 Lessons 1, 4, 5, 6, 7, 8, 11, 12, 13, 14, 15, 18, 19, 20; Unit 4 Lessons 1, 2, 3, 4, 5, 8, 10, 11, 16, 18, 19, 20; Unit 5 Lessons 3, 4, 7, 8, 9, 10, 12, 13, 14, 15, 16, 17, 18, 19, 20

Count to tell the number of objects.

K.CC.B.4	Understand the relationship between numbers and quantities; connect counting to cardinality.	Unit 1 Lessons 1, 2, 3, 4, 5, 6, 7, 9, 11, 12, 13, 14, 15, 16, 17; Unit 2 Lessons 1, 2, 3, 4, 5, 7, 8, 9, 10, 11, 15, 16, 19, 20; Unit 3 Lessons 1, 2, 4, 5, 7, 11, 13, 14, 15, 18, 19, 20; Unit 4 Lessons 1, 3, 4, 5, 6, 7, 10, 12, 15, 20; Unit 5 Lessons 2, 3, 7, 9, 13, 14, 15, 16, 17, 18, 19, 23
K.CC.B.4.a	Understand the relationship between numbers and quantities; connect counting to cardinality. • When counting objects, say the number names in the standard order, pairing each object with one and only one number name and each number name with one and only one object.	Unit 1 Lessons 1, 2, 3, 4, 5, 6, 7, 9, 11, 12, 13, 14, 15, 16, 17; Unit 2 Lessons 1, 2, 3, 4, 5, 11, 15; Unit 3 Lesson 2; Unit 4 Lessons 1, 4, 10, 12; Unit 5 Lesson 2

■ Major   ■ Supporting   ■ Additional

Common Core State Standards for Mathematical Content

K.CC Counting and Cardinality

K.CC.B.4.b	Understand the relationship between numbers and quantities; connect counting to cardinality. • Understand that the last number name said tells the number of objects counted. The number of objects is the same regardless of their arrangement or the order in which they were counted.	Unit 1 Lessons 1, 2, 3, 4, 5, 6, 7, 9, 11, 12, 13, 14, 15, 16, 17; Unit 2 Lessons 1, 2, 3, 4, 5, 7, 8, 11, 15; Unit 3 Lessons 2, 8, 11, 18; Unit 4 Lessons 1, 4, 10, 12; Unit 5 Lesson 2
K.CC.B.4.c	Understand the relationship between numbers and quantities; connect counting to cardinality. • Understand that each successive number name refers to a quantity that is one larger.	Unit 2 Lessons 1, 10, 12, 14, 16, 19, 20; Unit 3 Lessons 11, 12, 13, 14; Unit 4 Lessons 4, 5, 7, 12, 15; Unit 5 Lessons 5, 7, 9, 14, 15, 23
K.CC.B.5	Count to answer "how many?" questions about as many as 20 things arranged in a line, a rectangular array, or a circle, or as many as 10 things in a scattered configuration; given a number from 1–20, count out that many objects.	Unit 1 Lessons 1, 2, 3, 4, 5, 6, 7, 9, 11, 12, 13, 14, 15, 16, 17; Unit 2 Lessons 1, 2, 3, 4, 5, 7, 8, 9, 12, 13, 14, 15, 16, 17, 19, 20; Unit 3 Lessons 1, 2, 3, 4, 5, 6, 7, 8, 10, 11, 12, 13, 14, 15, 16, 17, 18, 19, 20, 21; Unit 4 Lessons 1, 2, 3, 4, 5, 6, 7, 8, 10, 11, 12, 13, 16, 18, 19, 20; Unit 5 Lessons 2, 3, 4, 5, 6, 7, 8, 9, 10, 11, 14, 15, 16, 17, 18, 19, 20

Compare numbers.

K.CC.C.6	Identify whether the number of objects in one group is greater than, less than, or equal to the number of objects in another group, e.g., by using matching and counting strategies.	Unit 1 Lessons 9, 11, 12, 13, 16, 17; Unit 2 Lessons 7, 9, 13; Unit 3 Lessons 10, 12; Unit 4 Lessons 10, 20; Unit 5 Lessons 1, 10, 14, 16, 17, 20
K.CC.C.7	Compare two numbers between 1 and 10 presented as written numerals.	Unit 1 Lessons 9, 15; Unit 2 Lessons 7, 9; Unit 3 Lessons 12, 14; Unit 4 Lessons 6, 10, 20; Unit 5 Lessons 16, 17, 20

■ **Major**   ■ **Supporting**   ■ **Additional**

K.OA Operations and Algebraic Thinking

Understand addition as putting together and adding to, and understand subtraction as taking apart and taking from.

K.OA.A.1	Represent addition and subtraction with objects, fingers, mental images, drawings, sounds (e.g., claps), acting out situations, verbal explanations, expressions, or equations.	Unit 1 Lessons 7, 8, 9, 11, 12, 13, 14; Unit 2 Lessons 2, 3, 4, 5, 6, 9, 10, 11, 12, 14, 15, 16, 19; Unit 3 Lessons 1, 3, 4, 5, 6, 7, 8, 11, 13, 15, 16, 17, 19, 20; Unit 4 Lessons 1, 2, 3, 4, 5, 6, 7, 8, 10, 11, 12, 13, 15, 16, 17, 18, 19, 20; Unit 5 Lessons 3, 4, 5, 6, 7, 8, 9, 10, 11, 12, 13, 14, 15, 16, 17, 18, 19, 20
K.OA.A.2	Solve addition and subtraction word problems, and add and subtract within 10, e.g., by using objects or drawings to represent the problem.	Unit 1 Lessons 7, 8, 14; Unit 2 Lessons 2, 3, 5, 6, 11, 12, 14, 15, 16; Unit 3 Lessons 1, 3, 4, 7, 11, 16; Unit 4 Lessons 1, 2, 3, 4, 6, 7, 8, 10, 11, 12, 13, 15, 16, 17, 18, 19, 20; Unit 5 Lessons 3, 4, 5, 6, 7, 8, 9, 10, 11, 12, 13, 14, 15, 16, 19
K.OA.A.3	Decompose numbers less than or equal to 10 into pairs in more than one way, e.g., by using objects or drawings, and record each decomposition by a drawing or equation (e.g., $5 = 2 + 3$ and $5 = 4 + 1$).	Unit 2 Lesson 2; Unit 3 Lessons 1, 3, 4, 6, 16, 17, 18; Unit 4 Lessons 2, 3, 4, 5, 7, 8, 11, 12, 13, 18, 19; Unit 5 Lessons 3, 4, 5, 6, 7, 8, 9, 10, 11, 12, 13, 14, 15, 16, 18, 19
K.OA.A.4	For any number from 1 to 9, find the number that makes 10 when added to the given number, e.g. by using objects or drawings, and record the answer with a drawing or equation.	Unit 4 Lessons 2, 4, 8, 11, 13, 18, 19; Unit 5 Lessons 3, 6, 8, 11, 12, 13, 15, 18, 19
K.OA.A.5	Fluently add and subtract within 5.	Unit 3 Lessons 4, 5, 6, 7, 12, 14, 18, 19; Unit 4 Lessons 3, 12, 15, 17; Unit 5 Lessons 7, 10

Common Core State Standards for Mathematical Content

K.NBT Number and Operations in Base Ten

Work with numbers 11–19 to gain foundations for place value.

| K.NBT.A.1 | Compose and decompose numbers from 11 to 19 into ten ones and some further ones, e.g., by using objects or drawings, and record each composition or decomposition by a drawing or equation (e.g., 18 = 10 + 8); understand that these numbers are composed of ten ones and one, two, three, four, five, six, seven, eight, or nine ones. | Unit 2 Lesson 10; Unit 3 Lessons 2, 3, 5, 6, 8, 13, 15, 17, 18, 19, 20; Unit 4 Lessons 3, 5, 7, 10, 12, 16, 18, 20; Unit 5 Lessons 1, 2, 3, 4, 5, 6, 7, 9, 10, 11, 15, 17, 18, 19, 20, 23 |

K.MD Measurement and Data

Describe and compare measurable attributes.

| K.MD.A.1 | Describe measurable attributes of objects, such as length or weight. Describe several measurable attributes of a single object. | Unit 5 Lessons 21, 22, 23 |
| K.MD.A.2 | Directly compare two objects with a measurable attribute in common, to see which object has "more of"/"less of" the attribute, and describe the difference. | Unit 5 Lessons 21, 22, 23 |

Classify objects and count the number of objects in each category.

| K.MD.B.3 | Classify objects into given categories; count the numbers of objects in each category and sort the categories by count. | Unit 1 Lesson 10; Unit 2 Lessons 13, 17; Unit 3 Lessons 10, 12, 21; Unit 4 Lessons 1, 9, 22 |

■ Major   ■ Supporting   ■ Additional

Common Core State Standards for Mathematical Content

K.G Geometry

Identify and describe shapes (squares, circles, triangles, rectangles, hexagons, cubes, cones, cylinders, and spheres).

K.G.A.1	Describe objects in the environment using names of shapes, and describe the relative positions of these objects using terms such as *above, below, beside, in front of, behind, and next to.*	Unit 1 Lessons 8, 10, 18; Unit 2 Lessons 13, 17, 20: Unit 3 Lessons 10, 12, 21; Unit 4 Lessons 9, 14, 21, 22; Unit 5 Lesson 13
K.G.A.2	Correctly name shapes regardless of their orientations or overall size.	Unit 1 Lessons 8, 10, 18; Unit 2 Lessons 13, 17, 20: Unit 3 Lessons 9, 10, 12, 21; Unit 4 Lessons 9, 14, 21, 22; Unit 5 Lesson 13
K.G.A.3	Identify shapes as two-dimensional (lying in a plane, "flat") or three-dimensional ("solid").	Unit 1 Lessons 8, 10, 18; Unit 2 Lesson 13; Unit 4 Lessons 9, 14, 21

Analyze, compare, create, and compose shapes.

K.G.B.4	Analyze and compare two- and three-dimensional shapes, in different sizes and orientations, using informal language to describe their similarities, differences, parts (e.g., number of sides and vertices/"corners") and other attributes (e.g., having sides of equal length).	Unit 1 Lessons 8, 10, 16, 18; Unit 2 Lessons 13, 17, 20; Unit 3 Lessons 10, 21; Unit 4 Lessons 9, 14, 21, 22
K.G.B.5	Model shapes in the world by building shapes from components (e.g., sticks and clay balls) and drawing shapes.	Unit 1 Lesson 10; Unit 3 Lesson 9; Unit 4 Lessons 9, 21
K.G.B.6	Compose simple shapes to form larger shapes.	Unit 3 Lesson 9; Unit 4 Lesson 21; Unit 5 Lesson 13

© Houghton Mifflin Harcourt Publishing Company

Common Core State Standards for Mathematical Practice

MP1 Make sense of problems and persevere in solving them.

Mathematically proficient students start by explaining to themselves the meaning of a problem and looking for entry points to its solution. They analyze givens, constraints, relationships, and goals. They make conjectures about the form and meaning of the solution and plan a solution pathway rather than simply jumping into a solution attempt. They consider analogous problems, and try special cases and simpler forms of the original problem in order to gain insight into its solution. They monitor and evaluate their progress and change course if necessary. Older students might, depending on the context of the problem, transform algebraic expressions or change the viewing window on their graphing calculator to get the information they need. Mathematically proficient students can explain correspondences between equations, verbal descriptions, tables, and graphs or draw diagrams of important features and relationships, graph data, and search for regularity or trends. Younger students might rely on using concrete objects or pictures to help conceptualize and solve a problem. Mathematically proficient students check their answers to problems using a different method, and they continually ask themselves, "Does this make sense?" They can understand the approaches of others to solving complex problems and identify correspondences between different approaches.

Unit 1 Lessons 8, 9, 10, 18
Unit 2 Lessons 1, 2, 3, 5, 6, 8, 10, 13, 15, 17, 20
Unit 3 Lessons 1, 4, 7, 16, 21
Unit 4 Lessons 2, 3, 4, 5, 6, 9, 10, 12, 14, 15, 21, 22
Unit 5 Lessons 1, 2, 4, 5, 10, 15, 16, 21, 22, 23

MP2 Reason abstractly and quantitatively.

Mathematically proficient students make sense of quantities and their relationships in problem situations. They bring two complementary abilities to bear on problems involving quantitative relationships: the ability to *decontextualize*—to abstract a given situation and represent it symbolically and manipulate the representing symbols as if they have a life of their own, without necessarily attending to their referents—and the ability to *contextualize*, to pause as needed during the manipulation process in order to probe into the referents for the symbols involved. Quantitative reasoning entails habits of creating a coherent representation of the problem at hand; considering the units involved; attending to the meaning of quantities, not just how to compute them; and knowing and flexibly using different properties of operations and objects.

Unit 1 Lessons 6, 11, 14, 16, 18
Unit 2 Lessons 2, 9, 20
Unit 3 Lessons 1, 3, 4, 10, 11, 12, 14, 21
Unit 4 Lessons 1, 2, 4, 5, 6, 7, 9, 12, 16, 17, 18, 19, 22
Unit 5 Lessons 7, 15, 17, 18, 20, 23

MP3 Construct viable arguments and critique the reasoning of others.

Mathematically proficient students understand and use stated assumptions, definitions, and previously established results in constructing arguments. They make conjectures and build a logical progression of statements to explore the truth of their conjectures. They are able to analyze situations by breaking them into cases, and can recognize and use counterexamples. They justify their conclusions, communicate them to others, and respond to the arguments of others. They reason inductively about data, making plausible arguments that take into account the context from which the data arose. Mathematically proficient students are also able to compare the effectiveness of two plausible arguments, distinguish correct logic or reasoning from that which is flawed, and—if there is a flaw in an argument—explain what it is. Elementary students can construct arguments using concrete referents such as objects, drawings, diagrams, and actions. Such arguments can make sense and be correct, even though they are not generalized or made formal until later grades. Later, students learn to determine domains to which an argument applies. Students at all grades can listen or read the arguments of others, decide whether they make sense, and ask useful questions to clarify or improve the arguments.

Unit 1 Lessons 1, 2, 3, 4, 5, 6, 9, 10, 11, 12, 14, 15, 17, 18
Unit 2 Lessons 1, 2, 3, 4, 5, 6, 7, 8, 9, 10, 11, 12, 13, 14, 15, 16, 17, 18, 19, 20
Unit 3 Lessons 1, 2, 3, 4, 5, 6, 7, 8, 9, 10, 11, 12, 13, 14, 15, 16, 17, 18, 19, 20, 21
Unit 4 Lessons 1, 2, 3, 4, 5, 7, 8, 9, 10, 11, 12, 13, 14, 15, 16, 17, 18, 19, 21, 22
Unit 5 Lessons 1, 2, 3, 4, 5, 6, 7, 8, 9, 10, 11, 12, 13, 14, 15, 16, 17, 18, 19, 20, 21, 22, 23

MP4 Model with mathematics.

Mathematically proficient students can apply the mathematics they know to solve problems arising in everyday life, society, and the workplace. In early grades, this might be as simple as writing an addition equation to describe a situation. In middle grades, a student might apply proportional reasoning to plan a school event or analyze a problem in the community. By high school, a student might use geometry to solve a design problem or use a function to describe how one quantity of interest depends on another. Mathematically proficient students who can apply what they know are comfortable making assumptions and approximations to simplify a complicated situation, realizing that these may need revision later. They are able to identify important quantities in a practical situation and map their relationships using such tools as diagrams, two-way tables, graphs, flowcharts and formulas. They can analyze those relationships mathematically to draw conclusions. They routinely interpret their mathematical results in the context of the situation and reflect on whether the results make sense, possibly improving the model if it has not served its purpose.

Unit 1 Lessons 1, 2, 3, 5, 7, 8, 9, 11, 12, 13, 14, 17, 18
Unit 2 Lessons 10, 11, 12, 14, 16, 17, 19, 20
Unit 3 Lessons 1, 4, 7, 21
Unit 4 Lessons 2, 4, 6, 8, 12, 14, 20, 21, 22
Unit 5 Lessons 3, 4, 5, 6, 7, 9, 10, 12, 13, 19, 23

Common Core State Standards for Mathematical Practice

MP5 Use appropriate tools strategically.

Mathematically proficient students consider the available tools when solving a mathematical problem. These tools might include pencil and paper, concrete models, a ruler, a protractor, a calculator, a spreadsheet, a computer algebra system, a statistical package, or dynamic geometry software. Proficient students are sufficiently familiar with tools appropriate for their grade or course to make sound decisions about when each of these tools might be helpful, recognizing both the insight to be gained and their limitations. For example, mathematically proficient high school students analyze graphs of functions and solutions generated using a graphing calculator. They detect possible errors by strategically using estimation and other mathematical knowledge. When making mathematical models, they know that technology can enable them to visualize the results of varying assumptions, explore consequences, and compare predictions with data. Mathematically proficient students at various grade levels are able to identify relevant external mathematical resources, such as digital content located on a website, and use them to pose or solve problems. They are able to use technological tools to explore and deepen their understanding of concepts.

Unit 1 Lessons, 14, 18
Unit 2 Lessons 4, 9, 19, 20
Unit 3 Lessons 5, 8, 9, 13, 20, 21
Unit 4 Lessons 5, 7, 9, 14, 20, 21, 22
Unit 5 Lessons 5, 6, 10, 19, 23

MP6 Attend to precision.

Mathematically proficient students try to communicate precisely to others. They try to use clear definitions in discussion with others and in their own reasoning. They state the meaning of the symbols they choose, including using the equal sign consistently and appropriately. They are careful about specifying units of measure, and labeling axes to clarify the correspondence with quantities in a problem. They calculate accurately and efficiently, express numerical answers with a degree of precision appropriate for the problem context. In the elementary grades, students give carefully formulated explanations to each other. By the time they reach high school they have learned to examine claims and make explicit use of definitions.

Unit 1 Lessons 1, 2, 3, 4, 5, 6, 7, 9, 10, 11, 12, 13, 14, 15, 16, 17, 18
Unit 2 Lessons 1, 2, 3, 4, 5, 6, 7, 8, 9, 10, 11, 12, 13, 14, 15, 16, 17, 18, 19, 20
Unit 3 Lessons 1, 2, 3, 4, 5, 6, 8, 9, 10, 11, 12, 13, 14, 15, 16, 17, 18, 19, 20, 21
Unit 4 Lessons 1, 2, 3, 4, 5, 7, 8, 9, 10, 11, 12, 13, 14, 15, 16, 17, 18, 19, 20. 21, 22
Unit 5 Lessons 1, 2, 3, 4, 5, 6, 7, 8, 9, 10, 11, 12, 13, 14, 15, 16, 17, 18, 19, 20. 21, 22, 23

Common Core State Standards for Mathematical Practice

MP7 Look for and make use of structure.

Mathematically proficient students look closely to discern a pattern or structure. Young students, for example, might notice that three and seven more is the same amount as seven and three more, or they may sort a collection of shapes according to how many sides the shapes have. Later, students will see 7×8 equals the well remembered $7 \times 5 + 7 \times 3$, in preparation for learning about the distributive property. In the expression $x^2 + 9x + 14$, older students can see the 14 as 2×7 and the 9 as $2 + 7$. They recognize the significance of an existing line in a geometric figure and can use the strategy of drawing an auxiliary line for solving problems. They also can step back for an overview and shift perspective. They can see complicated things, such as some algebraic expressions, as single objects or as being composed of several objects. For example, they can see $5 - 3(x - y)^2$ as 5 minus a positive number times a square and use that to realize that its value cannot be more than 5 for any real numbers x and y.

Unit 1 Lessons 1, 4, 5, 6, 7, 8, 9, 10, 17, 18
Unit 2 Lessons 2, 3, 4, 5, 7, 8, 12, 13, 14, 16, 17, 20
Unit 3 Lessons 2, 3, 5, 6, 7, 8, 9, 10, 11, 15, 16, 17, 21
Unit 4 Lessons 1, 2, 4, 5, 6, 7, 8, 9, 11, 12, 13, 14, 15, 16, 20, 21, 22
Unit 5 Lessons 3, 6, 7, 8, 9, 11, 13, 14, 15, 17, 18, 20, 23

MP8 Look for and express regularity in repeated reasoning.

Mathematically proficient students notice if calculations are repeated, and look both for general methods and for shortcuts. Upper elementary students might notice when dividing 25 by 11 that they are repeating the same calculations over and over again, and conclude they have a repeating decimal. By paying attention to the calculation of slope as they repeatedly check whether points are on the line through (1, 2) with slope 3, middle school students might abstract the equation $(y - 2)/(x - 1) = 3$. Noticing the regularity in the way terms cancel when expanding $(x - 1)(x + 1)$, $(x - 1)(x^2 + x + 1)$, and $(x - 1)(x^3 + x^2 + x + 1)$ might lead them to the general formula for the sum of a geometric series. As they work to solve a problem, mathematically proficient students maintain oversight of the process, while attending to the details. They continually evaluate the reasonableness of their intermediate results.

Unit 1 Lessons 4, 7, 10, 11, 14, 17, 18
Unit 2 Lessons 16, 19, 20
Unit 3 Lessons 4, 5, 6, 7, 8, 9, 10, 12, 13, 14, 15, 17, 18, 19, 20, 21
Unit 4 Lessons 5, 6, 7, 9, 13, 15, 22
Unit 5 Lessons 15, 16, 17, 18, 20, 23

Index

© Houghton Mifflin Harcourt Publishing Company

Index

G

Geometry. *See also* **Circle; Cone; Cube; Cylinder; Hexagon; Rectangle; Sphere; Square; Triangle.**
attributes, 226, 237
  corners, 225
  faces, 237, 259
  sides, 51–52, 94, 153, 225
in environment, 93, 112, 263
that roll/don't roll, 259
that stack/don't stack, 259
three-dimensional shapes
  attributes of, 226, 259
  compare with two-dimensional, 226, 242
  compose, 260–261
  cone, 226, 238, 259, 264
  cube, 226, 237, 238, 242, 259–260, 264
  cylinder, 226, 238, 259, 263–264
  position (above, behind, below, in front), 238
  solid, 226, 242
  sort, 226, 259
  sphere, 226, 242, 259, 263–264
two-dimensional shapes
  attributes, 153–154
  circle, 23–24, 31–32, 51–52, 54, 56, 93, 101–102, 105, 111–112, 185–186, 225–226
  combine, 93–94, 147–150
  compare with three-dimensional, 226
  compose, 147–150
  corners, 225
  flat, 226, 242
  hexagon, 101–103, 105, 150, 185–186, 226
  position (behind, below, beside, next to), 186
  rectangle, 29–32, 51–52, 54, 56, 93, 105, 111–112, 149, 153, 185–186, 225
  sort, 31–32, 51, 105, 111–112, 153–154, 159–160, 185–186
  square, 29–32, 51–52, 56, 91, 93–94, 101–103, 105, 112, 148–149, 153, 185–186, 225, 242
  trapezoid, 149
  triangle, 91–94, 101–103, 105, 111–112, 147–150, 153, 185–186, 225–226, 242

Groups
5-group, 65–66, 71–72, 95–96, 114, 117, 137, 143, 157, 163, 165, 166–167, 253
10-group, 145–146, 171–172, 251, 333, 337
comparing, 215, 227–228, 257, 308, 321, 329–332, 333, 341

H

Height
compare, 344

Hexagon, 101–106, 150

Hiding Zero Gameboard, 293–298

L

Length
compare, 343

M

Manipulatives
+/– Tiles, 63, 77–78
=/≠ Tiles, 63, 77–78
5-Counter Strips, 69–70
5-Square Tiles, 63–64
10-Counter Strips, 123–124

Index

Break-Apart Sticks, 213–214
Centimeter Cubes, 70
Circles, 21–22
Comparing Mat, 25, 27–28
Cylinder Pattern, 261–262
Fruit, 197–198
Hexagons, 101–102
Hiding Zero Gameboard, 293–298
At Home Number Cards, 135–136
Number Parade, 137, 143
Number Tiles, 5–6, 77
Shape Cards, 159–162
Sorting Cards, 151–152, 155–156, 159–162
Square-Inch Tiles, 5–6
Squares and Rectangles, 29–30
Stars, 277–278
Teen Equation Cards, 203–204
Teen Number Book, 243–244, 251–252, 255–256, 309–314
Teen Total Cards, 169–170
Triangles, 91–92
Vegetables, 199–200

Matching, 215–216, 227–228, 245, 257, 323

Math Mountain, 220, 230, 235, 303, 324, 327. *See also* **Tiny Tumblers.**

Math Stories. *See* **Addition; Subtraction.**

N

Nine. *See also* **Partners.**
groups of, 65, 67–68, 88
writing, 65, 88, 96, 107

Nineteen
tens in, 313
writing, 181

Number Parade, 137, 143

Numbers. *See also* **Teen Numbers.**
1 through 10, 5–6, 25, 38, 39, 41–42, 45, 50, 67–68, 77–78, 79–82, 82, 83, 84–85, 88, 95–96, 107–108, 109, 110, 137, 138, 157, 163, 165, 166–167
11 Through 20, 125, 138, 168, 180, 182, 205, 213–214, 221–222, 243–244, 251–252, 255–256, 283–285
comparing, 27–28, 33
ordering 1-10, 49, 61, 76, 82, 83–84, 107–108, 109, 110, 122
ordering 1-20, 125, 324
writing, 8, 37–38, 41–42, 50, 62, 71, 79–82, 83–85, 86, 95–96, 97–98, 107–108, 109, 110, 122, 131, 137, 138, 141, 142, 143, 165, 168, 171–172, 180, 182, 205, 221–222, 235, 289–290, 304, 308, 324

Number Tiles, 5–6, 77

O

One
count by, 27–28, 33–34, 45, 49, 61, 67–68, 71, 74, 76, 82, 85, 88, 95–96, 121–122, 125–126, 233, 239, 245, 247, 279, 286, 289–290, 304
writing, 37, 50, 55, 80, 81

P

Partners. *See also* **Math Mountain.**
of 2, 175
of 3, 175, 249, 253, 322
of 4, 129, 175, 249, 253
of 5, 129, 175, 179, 220, 249, 253, 299
of 6, 130, 137, 173, 176, 179, 217, 220, 235, 249, 253, 305, 322, 334

© Houghton Mifflin Harcourt Publishing Company

Index

Sphere
   describe, 259
   identify and name, 226, 242, 259, 263–264

Square, 29–32, 51–52, 105, 111–112, 148–149, 153, 185–186, 225

Square-Inch Tiles, 5–6

Story Problems, 43–44, 75, 87, 195

Strategy Check, 241–242, 301

Subtract
   fluency practice, 132, 138, 142, 164, 168, 180, 182, 206, 234, 240, 248, 300, 307, 320, 335–336, 338
   fluently within 5, 132, 138, 142, 143, 164, 168, 180, 182, 206, 234, 240, 248, 265–266, 300, 307, 320, 329–330, 335–336, 338, 350

Subtraction
   addition and, 43–44, 75, 87
   equations, 132, 138, 142, 143, 164, 168, 180, 182, 206, 234, 240, 248, 254, 265–266, 292, 300, 307, 320, 329–330, 335–336, 338, 350
   Fluency Check, 210, 224, 265–266, 287–288, 326–327, 350
   model
      drawings, 301
   represent problems, 99–100, 206
   story problems, 43–44, 75, 87, 301

Switched Partners, 176, 179, 334

Symbols
   +/− Tiles, 63–64, 77–78
   =/≠ Tiles, 63, 77–78
   equal sign (=), 63, 77, 163, 166–167, 307
   minus sign (−), 64, 78
   not equal to sign (≠), 64, 78, 163, 167, 307
   plus sign (+), 63, 77

T

Teen Equation Cards, 203–204

Teen Number Book, 243–244, 251–252, 255–256, 309–314

Teen Numbers, 138, 144, 168, 180, 181–184, 251, 275–276, 279, 333, 337
   partners, 171, 183–184, 205, 283–285
   writing, 138, 141, 144, 168, 171, 180, 182

Teen Total Cards, 133–134, 169–170

Ten, 201–202. *See also* **Partners.**
   count by, 289–290, 304
   groups of, 61, 66–68, 96, 97–98, 126, 285, 333
   writing, 66, 71–72, 96, 97–98

Ten-Counter Strips, 123–124

Ten-Groups, 145–146, 171–172, 251, 333, 337

Thirteen
   tens in, 311
   writing, 141

Three. *See also* **Partners.**
   groups of, 3, 7–8, 12–13, 18, 38–39, 40, 46, 48, 121
   writing, 38, 40, 50, 55, 80, 81

Three-dimensional shapes. *See* **Geometry.**

Tiny Tumblers, 220, 230, 235, 303, 324, 327

Totals
   partners, 327

Trapezoid, 149

Be an Illustrator

Illustrator: Josh Brill

Did you ever try to use shapes to draw animals like the seahorse on the cover?

Over the last 10 years Josh has been using geometric shapes to design his animals. His aim is to keep the animal drawings simple and use color to make them appealing.

Add some color to the seahorse Josh drew. Then try drawing a cat or dog or some other animal using the shapes below.

Shape Toolbox